# ENGAGING IN CONVERSATION ABOUT IDEAS IN TEACHER EDUCATION

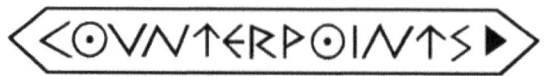

# Studies in the Postmodern Theory of Education

Joe L. Kincheloe and Shirley R. Steinberg
*General Editors*

Vol. 334

PETER LANG
New York • Washington, D.C./Baltimore • Bern
Frankfurt am Main • Berlin • Brussels • Vienna • Oxford

Fiona J Benson • Caroline Riches

# ENGAGING IN CONVERSATION ABOUT IDEAS IN TEACHER EDUCATION

PETER LANG
New York • Washington, D.C./Baltimore • Bern
Frankfurt am Main • Berlin • Brussels • Vienna • Oxford

Library of Congress Cataloging-in-Publication Data
Engaging in conversation about ideas in teacher education/
edited by Fiona J Benson, Caroline Riches.
p. cm. — (Counterpoints: studies in the postmodern theory of education, v. 334)
Includes bibliographical references.
1. Teachers—Training of. 2. Postmodernism and education.
I. Riches, Caroline. II. Title.
LB1707.B46   370.71'1—dc22   2008053498
ISBN 978-1-4331-0152-6 (hardcover)
ISBN 978-1-4331-0151-9 (paperback)
ISSN 1058-1634

Bibliographic information published by **Die Deutsche Bibliothek**.
**Die Deutsche Bibliothek** lists this publication in the "Deutsche
Nationalbibliografie"; detailed bibliographic data is available
on the Internet at http://dnb.ddb.de/.

© 2009 Peter Lang Publishing, Inc., New York
29 Broadway, 18th floor, New York, NY 10006
www.peterlang.com

All rights reserved.
Reprint or reproduction, even partially, in all forms such as microfilm,
xerography, microfiche, microcard, and offset strictly prohibited.

FOR JOE L. KINCHELOE

# Contents

INTRODUCTION
*Caroline Riches and Fiona J Benson* .................................................. 1

## THEME 1: PERSPECTIVES ON GOVERNANCE

American Educational Governance: Rights, Roles, and Responsibilities Meet Paradox and Challenge .................................................. 7
*Carolyn M. Shields*

Response:
*Peter P. Grimmett* .................................................. 20

The Governance of Canadian Teacher Education: A Macro-Political Perspective .................................................. 22
*Peter P. Grimmett*

Response .................................................. 33
*Carolyn M. Shields*

Questions for the Reader .................................................. 35

## THEME 2: EXPLORING THE LANDSCAPE OF TEACHER EDUCATION

The Teacher Education Landscape of My Imagining .................................................. 39
*Ruth Kane*

Response .................................................. 48
*Thomas Falkenberg*

Starting with the End in Mind: Ethics-of-Care-Based Teacher Education .................................................. 50
*Thomas Falkenberg*

Response .................................................. 60
*Ruth Kane*

Questions for the Reader ................................................................. 62

## THEME 3: THE QUALITY OF FIELD EXPERIENCE PROGRAMS

It Is Not Just Practice: Conflicting Goals, Unclear Expectations, Mixed Messages ............................................................................. 65
*Clare Kosnik*

    Response ................................................................................... 72
    *Jean-François Desbiens*

Practical Training Must Be More than Just Good Will in the Field ..... 74
*Jean-François Desbiens*

    Response ................................................................................... 79
    *Clare Kosnik*

Questions for the Reader ................................................................. 80

## THEME 4: RESPONDING TO DIVERSITY AND DEMANDS FOR SOCIAL JUSTICE

"This has nothing to do with us—or does it?" Youth as Knowledge Producers in addressing HIV and AIDS in a Canadian Preservice Education Program ......................................................................... 83
*Claudia Mitchell*

    Response ................................................................................... 93
    *Vianne Timmons*

Overcoming Barriers to Inclusivity: Preparing Preservice Teachers for Diversity .......................................................... 95
*Vianne Timmons*

    Response ................................................................................. 101
    *Claudia Mitchell*

Questions for the Reader ............................................................... 102

Contents ix

### THEME 5: IMAGINING SUSTAINABLE FUTURES FOR THE WORK OF TEACHERS

A New Thing in an Old World? Instrumentalism, Teacher Education, and Responsibility .................................................................. 105
*Anne M. Phelan*

    Response ................................................................................... 115
    *James Trier*

Subversive Engagements in Teacher Education ............................... 117
*James Trier*

    Response ................................................................................... 128
    *Anne M. Phelan*

Questions for the Reader ................................................................ 130

**AFTERWORD** .................................................................................. 131
    *Fiona J Benson and Caroline Riches*

**REFERENCES** .................................................................................. 133

# Introduction

*Caroline Riches and Fiona J Benson*

This book had its beginnings in a conference (*How Might Teacher Education Live Well in a Changing World?* Calgary, Alberta, 2006) dedicated to an exploration of necessary directions for teacher education. These directions were captured in five themes, the same five themes that form the structure and character of this book. The innovative design of the conference allowed more time for conversation than is usual at such gatherings. Invariably, those conversations in which we participated directly or heard about second hand, raised significant and persistent challenges around a complex array of notions about the purpose, role, and direction of teacher education in contemporary times. Invariably too, these conversations had to be curtailed far too quickly, leaving us, and we are sure others, with a nagging sense of illumination and promise cut short. This book then, is our attempt to reengage with and prolong these conversations and to encourage discussion with an even broader audience. It is our belief that the essays contained in this book will be of interest to teacher educators, teachers, researchers in the field, those engaged in graduate studies in education, policy makers, and other stakeholders in teacher education. There is something quite wonderful about the excitement and energy that is generated by the swirl of intense conversation between engaged minds, and this is what we hope this book will inspire.

One of the common laments in faculties of education (Benson & Riches, 2008; Darling-Hammond, 2006) is that there is a disconnect between theory and practice; we hear this time and again from students in teacher preparation programs as they move between theoretical, pedagogical, and even professional courses at the university and field experiences in the schools. It is our position that this divide also exists between graduate studies in education, dare we say in the "ivory tower," and teacher preparation programs. The purposes and outcomes of teacher education need to be infused with a deep responsibility to articulate and respond to the contemporary demographic, social, cultural, and economic challenges of the communities they serve. There needs to be a response to diversity, social justice, and consequent teaching and learning practices in schools. Such notions entail both a critical assessment of teacher education programs, as well as an imaginative reconceptualization of possibilities and the roles of stakeholders in teacher education and indeed education in (and for) contemporary times. This book strives to break down the silos of theory and practice, to discuss cutting-edge theories of education as they apply across teacher education that must include the critical nature of the preparation of teachers who educate our children. In constructing this book, we have sought out educational thinkers who have taken up these contemporary ideas and issues in education in considered and rational ways that are both grounded in reality and consider practical application. In dialogue and response dyads the authors grapple with one another as they debate cutting-edge ideas within five particular themes of concern to teacher education. As part of this process they pose questions to one another as well as to the reader as an invitation to enter their conversation. What follows is a brief introduction to the authors' thoughts as they engage with these important ideas.

In addressing the first theme, Perspectives on Governance, Shields makes a compelling case for why there needs to be a reform of certain of the structures that govern public education in America. She claims that "the education system [as it stands] is performing a reproductive rather than a transformative function" and proffers compelling insights into who controls education, and for what purpose. She shines a bright light on mechanisms of control and oversight such as standardization and funding, and in so doing, argues for a radically different redistribution of resources that takes into account local and regional differences that would transform education for everyone's benefit. Grimmett, for his part, argues against unwarranted interference from government into the governance of teacher education. He builds his argument by leading us through a skilful interpretation of three distinct phases of the evolution of the current professionalization or deregulation models in four of Canada's provinces: Québec, Manitoba, British Columbia, and Ontario. He posits that collaborative professional governance is the desirable venue for crafting a compelling vision for teacher education that serves the public good, rather than external political interference. He presents the reader with what he believes will be key challenges to what comprises professional knowledge and the protection of the public interest in teacher education governance across Canada.

Kane, speaking to the theme, Exploring the Landscape of Teacher Education, evokes the kinds of values, beliefs, and practices that should be critical to teacher education. Within the context of a shared vision of teaching and learning, she articulates the underlying foundations of a teacher education program based on principles that are ethically grounded and in so doing, places the student teacher's developing knowledge of self as teacher at the centre of the learning-to-teach process. Falkenberg takes this notion even further by embracing a "moral purpose of schooling" that suggests the central task of teacher education programs is to prepare teacher candidates as ethics-of-care-based agents. Kane and Falkenberg boldly inquire into the kinds of teacher education that might actively contribute to the impact of world change in ways that will also enable new teachers to "live well."

The Quality of Field Experience Programs, theme 3, is taken up by Kosnik and Desbiens as they deliberate the composition of effective field experiences in teacher education. Kosnik asks us to think about problems not typically considered in teacher education and the complexity of those problems. Engaging in that very process, she unpacks the conflicting goals and cross-purposes of the many stakeholders involved in the practicum, and in response to what is revealed, calls for a reconceptualization of the entire practicum component that must have, as its central focus, the pupils in the classroom. She argues that this shift in focus from student teacher to pupil would alter many of the problematic dynamics that play out within student teaching placements. Desbiens, too, is deeply concerned about the need to infuse the field experience with the dynamics he believes are most likely to result in an effective learning opportunity. His focus, however, is on the role the cooperating teacher plays in mentoring student teachers. He wrestles with the contradictions and challenges inherent in that role and in how that role is understood within teacher education. In so doing, he poses some serious questions to the reader about why so little energy is devoted to the training and supervision of those who are co-responsible for teacher preparation.

In theme 4, Responding to Diversity and Demands for Social Justice, Mitchell and Timmons exchange ideas about the value of preservice teachers confronting their own beliefs as a means toward developing a true awareness of these complex issues. In her essay, Mitchell argues that it is through encouraging youth as "knowledge producers" that the power of "starting with ourselves" is realized. She takes us into a university-based teacher education environment where preservice teachers consider their own responses and responsibilities specific to the global and local HIV and AIDS crisis, as both backdrop and foreground to taking up larger issues such as poverty, gender, and race. Timmons further emphasizes the importance of enabling engagement with issues of social justice and diversity in teacher education classes. With her focus on education for all, and the preparation of teachers for the complexities of the inclusive classroom, Timmons underlines that preservice teachers, and teacher educators, need to become conscious of their own biases and of the impact of their own attitudes. Mitchell and Timmons make a convincing case it is only through this self-awareness that transformation can occur at the level of the school curriculum, in the school classroom, and most important of all, for the students in the schools.

The concluding theme of this book considers notions around Imagining Sustainable Futures for the Work of Teachers. Phelan and Trier take up, from disparate sites of interrogation, how the research and work of teacher educators and teacher education might be renewed in order to move from a place of narrow scrutiny to one of radical possibility. Phelan asks us to grapple with the question, "Could teachers or teacher educators not be people with a 'revolutionary spirit,' who can keep alive the utopian moment in thinking that refuses to accept what presently exists as the measure of all reality?". She acknowledges that the necessary unease and bewilderment that questions such as this cause, are as important to the process of renewal as the questions themselves. Trier, in his quest to subvert the "old education," undertakes Postman and Weingartner's call for societal revolution as being, in part, the everyday actions that teachers can perform in practical ways on a small scale in their classrooms. He shares how, in a methods course he teaches, he creates situations in which preservice teachers engage with theory in ways that alter their familiar understandings by challenging their everyday perceptions. Both authors challenge the reader to consider how they make a difference and move teacher education forward to democracy and plurality.

The design of this book invites you, the reader, to enter into the dialogues from where you are presently positioned. The authors' intrepid questions on each of the book's themes offer a provocative inducement for you to indulge in spirited reflection and/or conversation around the issues raised. It is our hope and goal that this book will stimulate thinking, engender discussion, and embolden action.

**THEME 1**

# Perspectives on Governance

CONTRIBUTING AUTHORS
Peter P. Grimmett
Carolyn M. Shields

# American Educational Governance

## Rights, Roles, and Responsibilities Meet Paradox and Challenge

*Carolyn M. Shields*

The National Center for Education Statistics (NCES) calculated that in 2008, nearly 50 million students attended approximately 97,000 public elementary and secondary schools in approximately 15,000 districts throughout the United States (Institute of Education Sciences, n.d.). Levine, McLaughlin, and Sietsema (1996) reported that in 1990–1991, there were 15,358 regular school districts, with over half of them serving "fewer than 1,000 students" (p. xiii); additionally there were 1,336 other administrative units exercising some degree of control and oversight over education. No matter what else one chooses to say about the huge, complex, and multilayered system that governs education in America today, one indisputable aspect is that it exhibits neither equality nor equity. Moreover, the disparities are obvious in terms of resources—human, physical, or fiscal—and in terms of the quality of education offered to students, their opportunities to learn, and hence their possible life's chances beyond school.

The history of American education and governance are obviously topics too vast to be covered here; nevertheless, in this essay, I want to examine the question of who controls education. In so doing, I will provide a brief overview of some elements of educational governance that paradoxically purport to ensure a general level of access and appropriate education to all students, while, at the same time, perpetuating and reproducing educational inequities and posing significant challenges to those wanting to overcome them. I begin with a brief look at some federal and national forces, the role of states, and of local school boards. Although there is likely no "typical" state, here I use Illinois to illustrate some of the conundrums and paradoxes inherent in the system. I conclude by identifying some of the implications of this complex approach to governance for achieving both excellence and equity for all students.

Indisputably, educational benefits are unequally distributed in America. Some students (largely those whose families live in quite comfortable material circumstances) are very well served in our current education system. For the most part, these students live in relatively wealthy, upper- or middle-class neighborhoods or in the wealthier, more industrialized states. These are the students who perform well on standardized tests and whose test scores, as Berliner and Biddle demonstrated 15 years ago,[1] maintain the illusion that although the U.S.A. is not performing at the top of international comparisons, neither is it at the bottom. Moreover, of course, those with the means and desire to do so, always have the option of opting out of public education and sending their children to private schools. At the same time, many students are not as well served by public education in America. These are, for the most part, students whose material circumstances are less advantaged or whose home language and culture differ, sometimes in significant ways, from the mainstream. The formal structures or cultures of schooling also tend to marginalize some students and inhibit their ability to achieve their full potential, particularly those students who may differ in terms of appearance or sexual orientation. To explain how the U.S. (sometimes described as the "most innovative economy in the world," Bush, 2004, p. 121) has reached the point of what Miller (2008) calls "educational mediocrity" (p. 2), it is essential to understand some of the fundamental principles of education in the United States.

## Who Controls Education? A National Perspective

The preamble to the U.S. Constitution proclaims the desire to "form a more perfect union," "establish justice," "ensure domestic tranquility," "provide for common defence," "promote the general welfare," and "secure the blessings of liberty." Nowhere in the original Constitution is education mentioned. Under the provision of the 10th Amendment, education is a power reserved to the states or to the people. This does not mean there is no federal presence in American education, simply that each state has jurisdiction over educational matters within its boundaries. Some states,[2] such as Maryland, have chosen to bypass districts altogether and to govern school systems at the county level. Some (e.g., Florida) have districts corresponding to the number of their counties. Hawaii comprises a single statewide school district. Some

---

[1] They demonstrated that when U.S. scores were disaggregated, students from Iowa, North Dakota, or Minnesota performed with countries such as Taiwan and Korea (near the top) while students from Mississippi performed at the bottom, commensurate with students from Jordan (Berliner & Biddle, 1995, p. 60).

[2] Reliable data on school boards are difficult to find and, unless otherwise indicated, all data related to size are drawn from the online encyclopedia Wikipedia.

states have relatively fewer and larger districts (Nevada has 17, Utah 40), while others have numerous districts (Texas and California both have well over 1,000).

The U.S. Department of Education was created in 1980 by combining offices from several federal agencies. The department's website explains that its "mission is to promote student achievement and preparation for global competitiveness by fostering educational excellence and ensuring equal access" (n.d., p. 1). It goes on to explain that the department's 4,200 employees and $68.6 billion budget are dedicated to:

> establishing policies on federal financial aid for education, and distributing as well as monitoring those funds, collecting data on America's schools and disseminating research, focusing national attention on key educational issues, prohibiting discrimination and ensuring equal access to education. (p. 2)

Hence, it is clear that although education is governed by each state, there is still a substantial federal presence in the United States—a presence that, despite the stated goal of fostering excellence, appears, instead, to result in compliance with minimum standards and attainment of a minimal level of service or standards. Although there are many different federal programs that have either a direct or an indirect impact on education nationally, most are well known, and I provide only a few examples here. Title 1, one of the oldest and largest federal programs provides assistance to districts based on the proportion of low-income families. Title IX bans "sex discrimination" in schools in both academic and athletic programs and requires approximately equal spending on programs for male and female students. Federal legislation also governs, in part, bussing and integration of schools. Two major and well-known examples of major federal legislative mandates include the Elementary and Secondary Education Act, commonly known as No Child Left Behind (NCLB) and the Individuals with Disabilities Education Improvement Act of 2004 (IDEIA).

NCLB (2002) requires that each state establish standards for student achievement and school performance and authorizes numerous programs and provisions to address student needs so that all children achieve a certain common standard. It states:

> The purpose of this title [I] is to ensure that all children have a fair, equal, and significant opportunity to obtain a high-quality education and reach, at a minimum, proficiency on challenging State academic achievement standards and state academic assessments. (Title I, § 1001)

Unfortunately, in practice and in law, the need to attain minimum proficiency seems to have trumped the purpose of attaining a fair, equal, and high-quality education. The IDEIA legislation claims to protect "the rights of individuals with disabilities in programs and activities that receive federal funds" (U.S. DOE, 2007)—again with an unfortunate focus on minimum standards rather than quality (as we shall see later).

Beyond federal legislation, several other national associations and phenomena help to account for a national presence and a high degree of educational standardization throughout the country. The National Council for Accreditation of Teacher Education (NCATE), a coalition of over 30 member organizations, claims to be "the teaching profession's mechanism to help to establish high quality teacher, specialist, and administrator preparation" (NCATE, 2007, p. 5). It currently accredits over 632 colleges of education and has a presence in 50 partnerships (including 48 states, the District of Columbia, and Puerto Rico). NCATE's work focuses on the development of standards, including those for accrediting many programs including Teacher Education, Early Childhood Preparation, Elementary Education, and Educational Leadership, and for the accreditation of professional development schools. To gain a sense of the scope of NCATE's standards, one needs only to glance through each pertinent document.

As an example, the 2002 Standards for Advanced Programs in Educational Leadership comprise seven main headings, each with several subsections (NPBEA, 2002). They relate to areas such as building vision, promoting a positive school culture, managing operations and resources, collaborating with families and community members, acting with integrity, understanding the wider context, and engaging in promising performance activities such as internships. A closer examination of standard 6, requiring an understanding of the wider context, demonstrates both the scope and the limitations of the NCATE standards. It states: "Candidates who complete the program are educational leaders who have the knowledge and ability to promote the success of all students by understanding, responding to, and influencing the larger political, social, economic, legal, and cultural context." Candidates, who are expected to act as "informed consumers," must be able to explain and analyze social, economic, political, and legal elements of their context and be able to work within these contexts to promote the success of all students. Note that leaders are expected to "work within" rather than to challenge or reform the current system. Thus, the standards do not necessarily ensure that leaders are well prepared for the complexity and diversity of today's schools.

A controversy that arose in 2006 is illustrative. During a spirited debate over whether NCATE should include any reference to social justice, then-president Arthur Wise stated: "I categorically deny the assertion that NCATE has a mandatory "social justice" standard . . . We don't endorse political and social ideologies. We endorse academic freedom, and we base our standards on knowledge, skills and professional disposition" (Powers, 2006). He added that "NCATE had decided to eliminate references to "social justice" from its current glossary because "the term is susceptible to a variety of definitions." Wasley (2006), writing on the same day in the *Chronicle of Higher Education*, stated that:

> The National Council for Accreditation of Teacher Education won a key endorsement on Monday in its quest for continued federal approval of its accrediting power after announcing that it would drop controversial language relating to "social justice" from its accrediting standards for teacher-preparation programs. (p. A 13)

The decision was lauded by both Greg Lukianoff, president of the Foundation for Individual Rights in Education and Stephen Balch, president of the National Association of Scholars (Wasley). Following the resolution of this issue, NCATE's authority was recognized for an additional five years.

Failure to acknowledge that the endorsement of academic freedom is itself an expressed political and social ideology is emblematic of the problem. The assumption (and presumption) of neutrality in educational standards precludes discussion of differential approaches to address differing needs of students and their families. Moreover, this silence implicitly locates the responsibility or blame for shortcoming or failure on students and their families. By implication, the message is that the system, because of its "neutrality," and hence its comprehensive ability to serve all students, cannot be at fault.

Another major national presence in our education system deserving further attention is that of the teachers' unions—the American Federation of Teachers (AFT) and the National Educational Association (NEA). The former, the AFT, founded "in 1916 to represent the economic, social and professional interests of classroom teachers," is affiliated with the "international union of the AFL-CIO" that boasts a membership of "more than 3,000 local affiliates nationwide, 43 state affiliates, and more than 1.4 million members" (AFT, n.d. 1–2). The NEA says it is "the nation's largest professional employee organization, . . . committed to advancing the cause of public education. NEA's 3.2 million members work at every level of education—from preschool to university graduate programs. NEA has affiliate organizations in every state and in more than 14,000 communities across the United

States" (NEA, n.d., par. 1). Although there are obvious differences between the two organizations, related in part to their affiliations and mandates, it is clear that each exerts, through the comprehensive nature of its organization and membership and through extensive lobbying activities, a considerable influence on American education. Moreover, the NEA–AFT partnership, formed in 2001, combines the forces of the two organizations to work on behalf of their members to nurture and improve public education. As an example of their powerful influence, Gilford (2008, par. 2), no fan of teacher unions, reported that in the 2007–2008 fiscal year, the NEA spent $2.3 million "fighting a school voucher referendum in Utah." On the other hand, Petersen (2006), a long-time supporter of teacher unions, made the case that unions are helping teachers to "stand up against the de-skilling and straitjacketing effects of scripted curriculum". Regardless of one's position on either issue, the large membership and budgets of these two teacher unions create a powerful national force in educational policy and practice.

## Who Controls Education? A Local Perspective

From this discussion, it is apparent that although education comes under the purview of the states, there are substantial federal laws and national forces exercising some level of control over educational policies and practices. For example, given the foregoing, one might wonder if there is any substantive role in American education left to the states. States have the power (with federal approval) to prescribe what standards students will meet to comply with NCLB. In fact, states and school boards may also reject the norms of NCLB altogether if they also determine they can survive without the benefit of any federal funds. States may also develop graduation standards, specify and approve curriculum and textbooks, establish additional efforts and initiatives that should be emphasized in their schools, and of course, decide on appropriate levels of funding and funding protocols for public schools within their jurisdiction. In the 1990s, Kentucky initiated a statewide initiative related to portfolio assessment; in 2005 Utah determined it would forego federal funding to circumvent some of the restrictions of NCLB; and Illinois has mandated that all schools adopt a costly program, Response to Intervention (RTI), purported to maximize student achievement and reduce behaviour and management challenges.

Local control is further exhibited, of course, by the presence of locally elected school boards with the power to hire and fire educators, to bargain contracts related to teachers' salaries, provisions for special services and class sizes, and to determine spending priorities at the local level. The myriad activities and policies under the purview of local control result in considerable disparities in teacher salaries and training from one district and state to the next, in discrepancies in academic programs and expectations, and in dramatic inequities in spending and outcomes. Some would argue this suggests the national role is still too limited and that reform at the state level is not the answer. Miller (2008) emphasizes that local control creates a lack of uniformity that belies any significant understanding of how children are actually performing. He and others rightly argue that by leaving standards to each state, there is no criterion one can expect American children to achieve. This not only leaves the country vulnerable in international comparisons but also insists on the standardization of process, while leaving outcomes unaddressed.

## The Impact of Standardization

In the United States, education is typically described as a "public good" and seen as a desirable commodity. This perspective is reflective of the neoliberal argument that, once universal access has been achieved and standardization of outcomes adopted, education is a resource that can be managed to increase individual well-being, individual academic achievement, and ultimately, individual and national global competitiveness. In this (problematic) perspective, achievement gaps are a concern, not because of the system's failure to ensure that equal access translates into equitable outcomes for all students, but because America needs to maintain a global economic advantage. Children are seen as means to that end, as fungible items or widgets that must attain a designated common standard so that schools can achieve the uniform standard of "adequate yearly progress" (AYP).

To further illustrate the negative impact of this neo-liberal concept of education and of requiring only a minimum (and minimal) standard, we return to the IDEIA legislation, referred to earlier as a federal initiative to ensure educational access to students with disabilities. The 1982 Supreme Court ruling in *Board of Education v. Rowley* is still influential in determining the extent to which local authorities are expected to provide equitable education to all students (rather than to meet a simple minimum standard). The free appropriate public education (FAPE) statute, upheld in 1982 and in many subsequent decisions, did not require that a state "maximize the potential of handicapped children 'commensurate with the opportunity provided to other children'" (par. 4). In fact, in *Rowley*, the Supreme Court found that "the requirement that States provide 'equal' educational opportunities would thus seem to present an entirely unworkable standard requiring impossible measurements and comparisons" (par. 7). In sum, the finding required that students with special needs be provided with sufficient support and personalized services to permit them to benefit educationally from that instruction, but with no requirement that the benefit be equal to that of other children, or sufficient to maximize their potential.

Thus, on the basis of this brief overview of the current state of governance of American education, one could argue that neither federal legislation nor states' interpretations of their responsibilities results in equalized educational opportunities or achievement for all students. Neither the federal standard nor its interpretation by states or school boards requires an equitable distribution of educational goods and services to all children. As *Rowley* shows, legislation and policy continue to justify inequitable educational provisions. Nevertheless, I am not arguing for the elimination of minimum standards here, but simply positing the desirability of either higher standards than currently exist or the addition of new standards focusing on equity.

Because of the emphasis on minimal standards and the multiple layers of governance in our current system, American schooling fails, in large part, to act as a vehicle for social mobility and democratic advancement. The notion that education is a true public good therefore disintegrates. Instead, education exercises a largely reproductive function, through which middle- and upper-class forms of social, cultural, and economic capital are legitimated and other forms of capital are marginalized and devalued, thus continuing to do violence to students from other than typical middle-class families. The well-known "achievement gaps" between children from poverty and those from more advantaged homes, and between White, African American, and Hispanic youth only represent a small part of the picture of disparity in the United States. Clearly, these achievement gaps also help to perpetuate inequitable social and living conditions. Differential rates of health and well-being, of insurance coverage, of incarceration, and of poverty and wealth between and among certain groups—all tell the tale of a country in which there is continued reluctance to consider the need for policies that redress the widening gap between rich and poor. Moreover, there is need for a civic consciousness in which such redress and even redistribution is not seen simply as a penalty against those who work hard and are able to succeed, but a way of creating a viable democracy in which all citizens are valued and in which all work to the mutual benefit of the society as a whole.

## Who Funds Education and with What Results?

Perhaps nowhere are the disparities related to the challenges of complex layers of responsibility more noticeable, or the outcomes more distressing, than in the details of education funding in the United States. As I write this reflection on the governance of education in the United States, the momentous

2008 federal election is just around the corner. Still ringing in my ears is the oft-repeated sentiment, usually used, not as a goal, but as a way of ridiculing any change from the current neo-liberal system: "Spread the wealth around? Absolutely not!" International data inform us that the United States spends more on education (per pupil and in terms of percentage of GNP) at the P/K–12 level and in higher education than do any other G-8 nations. However, OECD (2004) reports indicate that American achievement falls well below countries that spend much less overall. In fact, in the 2003 mathematics assessment, U.S. students achieved below the 24th and 28th rank out of 41 countries—a range that represents statistical variation (p. 354). In addition to this midrange achievement, when both achievement and social equity are considered, the U.S. is considered to have relatively low equity—well below what might be anticipated when the total per pupil expenditure to age 15 of $80,000 is taken into account (p. 358).

When scores are disaggregated, as demonstrated nearly 15 years ago by Berliner and Biddle (1995), inequities in achievement among states are still greater, in some cases, than differences among countries. Rothstein (2000) provided an extensive overview of education funding in which he assessed states' overall fiscal effort and, again, identified dramatic differences among and within states. It is important here to note that federal assistance does little to remediate the situation and in some instances may "exacerbate it" (Rothstein, 2000, p. 57). The total estimated education expenditure for all U.S. public schools during the 2005–2006 school year was about $571.9 billion (NEA, 2008). Of this total, about 8.8 percent, or roughly $50.3 billion, came from the federal government (through programs supporting free and reduced lunch, bilingual aid, Title 1 programs, and so forth). However, federal funds did not and do not compensate for some states' disadvantages in funding education, and they certainly do not compensate for within-state disparities caused by local control of education funding.

When one examines Rothstein's analysis of states' per pupil expenditures for the 1996–1997 school year, the average across all states was $6,081, but the range, even when adjusted for regional cost differences, told a disturbing story of disparity. First-ranked New Jersey averaged $9,667 per pupil, while last-ranked Mississippi spent $3,704. In 2007-2008, New Jersey still ranked first in expenditures ($15,374), with Idaho the lowest at $7,305 per pupil (NEA, 2008). Rothstein argues that "a truly equitable school spending regime would dedicate more resources to disadvantaged than to other children" (p. 44). Moreover, to achieve equity, states with the greatest need (i.e., with the greatest percentage of disadvantaged children) would have to spend more of their own resources on education—a situation that is contrary to current practice. Unfortunately, Rothstein reports little equity in the system and concludes that the ideal situation, in which states with the greatest need would also have the greatest capacity to respond, does not exist. The issue is further exacerbated by internal inequities due to the historically heavy reliance in the U.S. on local property taxes to fund education.

Most states have taken steps to create more equality by establishing a base level of funding—a minimum level that, if not met at the local level, will be supplemented by the state. However, unless all districts or regions of a state share a relatively uniform level of property tax revenue (with similar percentages of high- and low-cost areas, high- and low-income neighborhoods, and similar population densities per school, etc.), funding within states will be—and definitely is—inequitable. In 2005, Kozol reported that in the Chicago area, the highest per pupil expenditures of $17,291 were in the Highland Park and Deerfield districts, with 90% White populations and only 8% low-income students. Meanwhile in Chicago itself, with 85% low-income students and 87% Black and Hispanic, the per pupil expenditure was $8,482 (p. 312). In like fashion, Kozol reported a $17,261 per pupil expenditure in Lower Merion, Pennsylvania, where less than 10% of the population in 2005 was Black or Hispanic and only 4% were low income. This was compared to Philadelphia where 71% of students lived in poverty, 79% were either Black or Hispanic, and the per pupil expenditure was $9,299.[3]

Approaches to education funding based on local control and state policies have been challenged repeatedly. On the basis of the equity of a state's education funding, 43 states have undergone lawsuits. Of these, the plaintiffs won 26 cases and the states themselves (i.e., the defendants) won 19. Verstegen (2007) reports that since 1989 there has been a shift in emphasis, with the focus changing to adequacy rather than equity. She and Driscoll explain, "Finance systems can be equitable but not adequate if children and youth within a state receive insufficient funding to meet state standards, requirements, and laws" (Verstegen & Driscoll, 2008, p. 341). Thus, states have again been forced to defend their approaches, this time with respect to whether or not they have adequately funded education. Early in 2007, 12 of these cases were undecided, with the plaintiffs having won in 20, and the defendants in 7. Although these cases have not determined a clear direction for future education spending, there is little doubt that fiscal disparities result in the unequal distribution of the "public good" of education and contribute to the need for ongoing costly social programs to redress the outcomes of the inequity.

---

[3] Paragraph taken from Shields, 2009, p. 79.

## The Impact of Local Control

Illinois provides a useful example of the impact of locally controlled educational spending. The fifth largest state in the U.S. by population (with almost 13 million people), Illinois has the nation's third highest number of school districts (behind Texas and California). The largest of the 873 districts, Chicago Public Schools—governs over 600 schools and 400,000 students and is one of only four Illinois districts with over 25,000 students. Of the rest, 450 districts have fewer than 1,000 students, and of these, 130 have fewer than 300 students being educated in 3,890 schools. The Illinois State Board of Education (ISBE, 2006) reports that for the 2005 school year, the base level of spending was $4,964 per pupil, with about 56% of this coming from local property taxes, 34% from state funds, and 10% from federal programs (p. 28).

Differences in regional wealth and hence local "ability to pay," however, result in wide variations from the average. The Illinois Board of Education reported that the average teacher salary for the 2007 school year was $56,640. Averages, however, may mask great disparities; for example, salaries for beginning teachers with a BA and no experience ranged from $22,079 to $48,200, while top Illinois teacher salaries exceeded $120,000 (ISBE, 2008). A similar range was to be found for administrators, with the highest paid superintendent receiving in excess of $385,000 and over 30 others receiving in excess of $250,000—all well above the state's published administrator average salary for 2006 of $100,431.

Although salaries do not tell the whole story, it becomes apparent that the quality of education offered to students in schools across the state, as determined by teacher certification and standards, curricular resources, and per pupil expenditure, varies considerably. Verstegen and Driscoll (2008) conclude in their study of the current state of Illinois' education funding that

> Large and growing inequalities characterize the school finance system in the state. The property tax is the decisive force in shaping inequalities, and "savage" inequalities characterize school funding in Illinois. Inequalities—amounting to $16,600 per pupil—are linked to local wealth rather than the wealth of the state as a whole. This makes the quality of a child's education a function of the wealth of his or her parents and neighbors and erodes educational opportunity. (p. 350)

Supporting education through property taxes is a key element of a governance system that identifies minimum standards but in which parental wealth and status too often determine the quality of education a child will receive.

## Conclusion

In a political system as large and complex as the American public education system, it is difficult to claim that reform of the governance structures would lead to greater equity. There does need to be a government presence to ensure minimum standards of education for all—although more detailed guidance about the content and level of the desired standards and more emphasis on high quality and equity are in order. Given the long history of, and belief in, local control, increasing the federal presence would likely be met with resistance and backlash. Yet, through this brief examination of the impact of local control on school funding, we have also seen that simply increasing the powers of state and local governments is unlikely to remediate the situation.

On the one hand, one barrier to more equitable and excellent education for all seems to be that of public will. Too often state and local governments look to the people, through referenda, for "permission" or willingness to change. Too often, bills asking for new funding for schools or consolidation of school districts fail because the request is not seen as in the interests of those who benefit from the status quo or those who currently have political and socioeconomic power to implement change. On the other hand, another barrier to improving education for all children inheres in any governance approach that purports to be neutral and perpetuates the myth that access to education through one's neighborhood school is the basis for equity and excellence. Those who govern education in the United States must begin to take local and regional differences (including ethnicity, income, and wealth) into account. Moreover, although disparity and inequity must be overcome, differences themselves should not be seen as problems but as realities that must guide the creation of new high-quality curriculum, pedagogy, and standards.

The conclusion is inescapable. At present, the partnership of federal, state, and local boards and the numerous organizations that exercise control over American education has created an educational system that falls far short of facilitating the "Great American Dream": equity and equality for all. Minimum federal standards do not set a high-enough bar, but neither does local control result in a more equitable or excellent education system. When the wealth of one's parents, or the color of one's skin, or the place one lives, or the language one speaks at home are the deciding factors in the quality of education a child receives, it is reasonable to claim that the education system is performing a reproductive rather than a transformative function. Change is needed to ensure that the windows of understanding opened in one's formative school years truly lead to a future of opportunity for all children,

Those who govern America's education system are abrogating their responsibility to improve the quality of education for all students. Our system, based on standardization of a minimum nature and denial of the inherently political and value-laden nature of the enterprise, is failing many of our children. The solution lies in a new political mind-set—one that looks to redistribution of resources and that recognizes that, in a democracy, high-quality education for all must not only be everyone's responsibility but must also work to everyone's benefit. As long as the goal is improvement rather than transformation, American education will continue down the path of mediocrity. When transformation becomes the guiding principle, we will have the opportunity to redress our "society of unfulfilled promises" (Greene, 1998, p. 5). We will begin to acknowledge that equal access, minimum standards, and minimal funding are insufficient to effect the change we need—a change that will ensure education becomes a true public good. We will begin to demand, not only new forms of governance but also new guiding principles; not simply foundation funding, but equity and adequacy of fiscal support for education; not simply minimal standards for access and services, but high standards for excellence in both inputs and outcomes. Education must be conceived, not as the basis for individual economic advancement, but as bedrock for a more equitable civil society. Only then will we enjoy the prospect of a brighter future for individuals, communities, and society as a whole—a future of hope for promises fulfilled.

# RESPONSE

*Peter P. Grimmett*

My colleague, Carolyn Shields, claims that the present partnership between and among federal, state, and local authorities that controls American education has essentially created a system that fails to provide equality and equity for all students. She documents the struggle between executive federalism and local state control that has taken place in the States since 1980 to show that reform of the governance structures would do little to address the need for greater equity in enhancing the life chances of children. Rather than seeing the governance of education in the U.S.A. as problematic, she suggests that a fundamental barrier to equity is a lack of public will to bring it about. Public will is expressed in policies. Policies, in turn, determine structures. Hence, her argument is that there is a need for fresh policies that address the need for greater equity in American education by taking the system beyond mere reproduction toward a transformative set of principles. But, while she ends with the indication that people will begin to demand new principles that will lead to new forms of governance, her essay is "thinnest at its sharpest end" in the sense that she does not articulate what such principles would look like.

In making her case about education not moving toward equity, Carolyn suggests "education is typically described as a public good and as a desirable commodity." Here, she is suggesting that this neo-liberalist policy is mere political rhetoric that leads to a serious diminution of the provision for equality and equity. I could not agree more. However, her proposed solution that a new political mind-set will bring about the needed transformation needs a great deal of amplification. What, for example, if the new political mind-set regards education as a public good but fails to understand that this does not necessarily equate with public education? All too often, there is a common belief that public education is always and automatically a public good. I want to argue that it is not intrinsically so, that it is far more complex, and that this belief serves to conceal the extensive role education plays in producing and distributing private goods,[1] a point that market-oriented consultants and policy makers typically emphasize. Likewise, in the case of public and private institutions, the ownership of the institution does not determine its nature. Private institutions can produce public goods and public institutions may produce private goods. In all cases, it is the *practice* of education that reveals the underlying purpose. Worldwide, the practice of education has become more and more dominated by the pursuit and enhancement of individual status goods. In neo-liberalist terms, the outcomes of education are designed to produce an economic advantage to the individual that can be exchanged in the marketplace.

But it need not be so. With Carolyn, I wish to see an education system that works toward greater equity but, to do so, requires public policies and institutional practices that reinforce education as a non-rivalrous and non-excludable public good. This is what must constitute a new political mindset, because the principles that structure the governance of education determine the nature of the goods produced. The problem facing education in a globalized world is that the neo-liberal agenda ensures that current outcomes are understood primarily through the market environment and therefore within the context of global *private* goods. Any solution must find ways of countering policies that have been framed by neo-liberalist values because those very values militate against the pursuit of equity.

---

[1] Here I am using Marginson's (2007b) distinction between public and private goods. Public goods are those that are subject to non-rivalry or non-excludability, and broadly available across populations, on a global scale (p. 315). A good is considered non-rivalrous if one person's use of it does not diminish another person's use. A good is considered non-excludable if a person cannot be prevented from using the good. Positional goods, or status goods, those that benefit the individual, are private goods.

# The Governance of Canadian Teacher Education

## A Macro-Political Perspective

*Peter P. Grimmett*

### Introduction

In Canada, teacher education is a provincial jurisdiction. Despite the cultural, ethnic, and linguistic diversity across Canada, all provinces have taken considerable interest in the preparation of teachers. In all provinces, a professional teaching certificate is normally issued to graduates of university preservice preparation programs. Most Canadian teachers therefore possess a first degree. The governance of teacher education falls under the provincial government except in British Columbia and Ontario where the British Columbia College of Teachers (BCCT) and the Ontario College of Teachers (OCT), respectively, act as professional self-regulating bodies that control certification and establish professional standards.

How did this state of affairs come about? Since 1960, there have been three periods of teacher education governance in Canada (Grimmett, 2008). The first (1960–1980) was characterized by benign government control where teacher education was regarded as training. The second (1980–2000) involved a move toward institutional governance where teacher education was viewed as learning to teach. The current period (1990–2010) is characterized by a policy context that has emphasized both professionalization and de-regulation, leading to governance by professional self-regulation or direct government control. I explore the macro-political pressures that have brought the teacher education policy context to the current period. The purpose is to show how these pressures have affected the way in which the dominant features of the current phase—professionalization and de-regulation—have evolved in four of Canada's provinces, Québec, Manitoba, British Columbia (BC), and Ontario. In two of the major anglophone provinces, Ontario and British Columbia (BC), there has been a move toward professional self-regulation, whereas the francophone province has adopted a form of governance that is one step removed from direct government control, and the prairie province constitutes an example of institutional governance that is marked by increased professional involvement and specific government control. My thesis is that the governance of teacher education across Canada will be subject to considerable change in the next decade or so, particularly as it becomes the site of contestation over what constitutes professional knowledge and protecting the public interest.

What forces, then, have been at work over the past 20 to 30 years that now affect the governance of teacher education in Canada? Examining the macro-political setting will shed light on this question.

## A Macro-Political Perspective[1]

The macro-political setting of the current period is neo-liberalism, which has led to the decline of the nation-state. Previously, under liberalism—where the individual was characterized as having autonomy and could practice freedom, and the role of government was to protect individual freedom—universities were central to the development of the nation-state.

Neo-liberalism is an outgrowth of liberalism in that it similarly emphasizes the primacy of the individual. It differs, however, in that it sees a role for the private sphere to expand to create more efficient market transactions in the public sphere. Public goods and services are re-defined as commodities that can be more effectively delivered through private sector competition. The state manages this through third-party evaluative regulatory structures that operate at arm's length from the state to ensure the efficiency and effectiveness of scarce public resources and remove the potential for inefficiency caused by political interference or lack of accountability. It is no surprise, then, that during the current period of neo-liberalist de-regulation we have seen the emergence of professional regulatory bodies.

The neo-liberal framework had its beginnings in the first period (1960–1980) and gained increasing influence during the first part of the second period (1980–2000). But it has become hegemonic since the fall of the Berlin Wall in 1989 and the fall of the Soviet Union in 1991 (Readings, 1996; Dale, 2005) that led to the discrediting of the alternate competing modern socio-political system epitomized by a Marxist economic framework. As neo-liberalism became the dominant discourse, there has been no effective alternative to counter its apparent pervasive influence, because we have come to believe that the ways of neo-liberalism are common sense and inevitable. Hence, neo-liberal thought has been able to extend its hegemonic socio-

---

[1] I am grateful for the stimulating ideas that Lane Trotter has shared with me on this subject.

economic reach into the public sphere to redefine roles and responsibilities in education, health care, and social welfare in terms of their economic utility (Fitzsimmons, 2000; Davies & Bansel, 2007).

Until the end of the cold war, universities were protected from the direct influence of neo-liberalism because they were bastions of cultural reproduction designed to counter external threats such as the Soviet Bloc (Readings, 1996). The change from liberalism to neo-liberalism has had profound consequences for universities. The privileged position the universities previously enjoyed has eroded, and they are now regarded as another appendage of the state social welfare apparatus. The traditional role of universities in knowledge formation and cultural reproduction is no longer central to the nation-state. Rather, it has been re-fashioned around academic capitalism to support economic development and global competitiveness. One consequence is that faculty is now seen as a group of self-interested individuals, undermining the notion that they act with professional responsibility. That is, the capacity for self-governance through collegial decision-making is seen as an anathema to the effective use of public funds. This is at odds with the modernist relationship between the nation-state and the university that supported professional responsibility and self-governance as a form of delegated authority to bodies possessing expertise.

Previously, "professionality" was seen to support the public good because it added to our understanding of what it means to be human (MacIntyre, 1997). Neo-liberalism rejects such a premise, viewing professionality as benefiting an elite few at the expense of the majority. Instead, neo-liberalism promotes "governmentality"—the end goals of "freedom," "choice," "competition," and so on are government constructions that are continuously monitored by "new management" technocrats, and represent not a retreat from government intervention but a re-inscription of particular techniques required for the exercise of government. In this way, freedom as a form of dissent, critique, and debate is re-defined as compliance, consumption, and productivity. Such a state of affairs lionizes economic rationality where individuality is discovered not in community but only in relation to market fulfillment; that is, the state *creates* individuals who are enterprising and competitive entrepreneurs. Consequently, the nation-state has been supplanted by supranational entities, for example, the Organization for Economic Cooperation and Development (OECD), the World Bank, and so on, which exist to provide both socio-economic political stability and harmonization.

While the decline of the nation-state has not yet become its own outright demise, its decline has nevertheless led to a trend toward standardization and instrumental rationality, which in turn is fostering deprofessionalization. In Europe, we have the Bologna Agreement, in Canada the Agreement for Internal Trade (AIT), labour mobility agreements that supersede any attempt to establish professional standards in local jurisdictions. How, then, does this affect university-based teacher education and its governance?

## Implications for the Governance of Canadian Teacher Education

Conducting teacher education in university settings is not straightforward. Neo-liberalist economic rationalist pressure makes university-based teacher education programs susceptible to academic drift as a result of teacher educators attempting to gain credibility in a research-intensive setting. This creates tensions because, in seeking to adopt the values of research-intensive academics, university teacher educators sometimes forget their ontological roots in practice. Have Canadian teacher educators successfully established their legitimacy in a research-intensive environment that enables them to tout their uniqueness as educators of teachers? The work of Cole (1999, 2000a, 2000b) suggests that gaining legitimacy in the university research environment has overshadowed the need to emphasize the distinctive contribution of teacher education. Consequently, the policy context in Canadian teacher education has moved in most provinces beyond the era of institutional governance (because universities were seen as acting out of self-interest) to an emphasis on (1) a return to government control (e.g., CAPFE in Québec), (2) a neo-liberalist constrained vestige of institutional governance (e.g., Manitoba), or (3) professional governance (e.g., the professional self-regulatory bodies in British Columbia and Ontario). This change in the policy context appears to have increased the susceptibility of teacher educators to external pressures.

## A Return to Government Control: The Case of CAPFE in Québec

In 1992, the province of Québec created the Comité d'Agrément des Programmes de Formation à l'Enseignement (CAPFE). CAPFE became an official organization responsible for the governance of teacher education when the Education Act was sanctioned on December 19, 1997. CAPFE accredits teacher education programs in the province and reports directly to the Minister of Education. This ostensibly independent committee is made up of nine members appointed by the Minister. Four are academics, four are teachers, plus one chair, alternately an academic, then teacher, and so on. Currently, discussions are underway to make the chair always an academic, that is, five academics, four teachers. One of the four representatives must be anglophone, to match the 25 percent representation of anglophones in Québec. CAPFE also has a full-time Secretary-Coordinator and one Ministry Observer. Accreditation panels have four members, all taken from the committee. Anglophone members head up site visits to anglophone programs. Francophone members lead site visits to francophone programs.

CAPFE develops tools, evaluation criteria, and methods to study teacher preparation programs. While respecting the freedom of action of the university, CAPFE can approve different and original preparation methods, insofar as they respect the guidelines of the Ministère de l'Éducation (MEQ). This dimension is crucial and goes to the very heart of its mandate. CAPFE is answerable only to the Minister of Education when it comes to accrediting teacher education programs and recommending programs that lead to teaching certification. Under the Education Act, CAPFE has a mandate to accredit teacher education programs according to how effectively the program allows the development of the professional competencies determined by the Minister and set out in the official teacher education guides.[2] Put differently, CAPFE must assure the Minister that an accredited program satisfies ministerial requirements. To this end, CAPFE has drawn upon its expertise and experience to develop writing guides for universities that wish to submit a program.[3] It has also developed evaluation grids for its own task of examining programs.

All teacher education programs in Québec are analyzed and evaluated for conformity with the following government-specified parameters:

- inclusion of means to address the two general orientations of teacher education, namely, teaching from a cultural perspective and increased professionalization
- compliance with exit profiles
- development of the professional competencies required of future teachers
- deep, ongoing concern for the quality of the language of instruction and second languages
- strong consideration given to the Québec Education Program at both the elementary and secondary levels
- reflection of the major changes in education in Québec and compliance with the various policies of the Ministère de l'Éducation, du Loisir et du

---

[2] http://www.capfe.gouv.qc.ca/accreditation.htm#1
[3] http://www.capfe.gouv.qc.ca/accreditation.htm#2

Sport, such as the curriculum reform, the policy on the evaluation of learning, and the policy regarding the integration of students with difficulties

—(http://www.capfe.gouv.qc.ca/accreditation.htm#1)

Thus, a third-party independent committee that is directly accountable to the provincial government is responsible for the Québec system of teacher education governance. This constitutes thinly veiled direct (and hardly benign) government intervention, in that government determines all committee appointments and accreditation parameters.

The experience of government control of teacher education in England would suggest that this change could have unfortunate consequences for protecting the public interest. For example, Ball (2003) has shown how the stringent British accountability approach has produced unexpected and undesirable outcomes:

> What is produced [under government control] is spectacle, or game playing, or cynical compliance, or what we might see as 'enacted fantasy' which is there simply to be seen and judged—a fabrication . . . The heart of the educational project is gouged out and left empty. Authenticity is replaced by plasticity. (Ball, 2003, pp. 222, 225)

To date, there is little research on the effect of CAPFE in the province of Québec. What is nevertheless clear is that its approach to the governance of teacher education differs from that practiced in Manitoba where academics engaged in teacher education appear to work in a model that represents a hybrid between and among institutional governance, collaboration with both the profession and government, and government control.

## Institutional Governance in Manitoba:[4] A Changing State of Affairs?

Although the Manitoba Education Administration Act (1987) made programs subject to the approval of the Minister for certification purposes, the powers of government control were largely benign and teacher education in the province was given to institutional governance. For instance, the University of Manitoba (the largest teacher education program in the province) redesigned its program between 1990 and 1993 without being required to consult with the government or the profession (Young, Hall & Clarke, 2007). The government's *Renewing Education: New Directions—A Blueprint for Ac-*

---

[4] This section draws on Young & Grimmett (2008).

*tion* (Manitoba Education and Training, 1994), however, heralded the beginning of intervention. The legal authority was established for the government to impose changes on teacher education programs, but there appears to have been little political will to do so. The Board of Teacher Education and Certification (BOTEC), consisting primarily of academics and some teachers that the government had established in 1965 during Phase 1, continued to act as a filter of government direction. Specifically, BOTEC was an important check on government attempts to conduct a broad-ranging review of teacher education with a view to establishing standardized programs across the province and a clearly defined set of standards for beginning teachers. Hence, Manitoba is a province that currently hangs on to a form of institutional governance, but it is a form that is essentially a hybrid of institutional governance marked by increased professional involvement and specific government control.

The government's announcement of new requirements for certification in 1998 and its subsequent replacement of BOTEC with the Teacher Education and Certification Committee (TECC) in 2000 confirmed the Manitoba government's desire to assert more control. TECC consisted of 12 members, six from the Manitoba Teachers' Society, four appointed, and only two university representatives. Unlike the councils of professional self-regulation bodies, members of the teaching profession in TECC are not elected but appointed. Even though it is not legally constituted as a third-party evaluative regulatory structure that operates at arm's length from government (as is the case in professional self-regulation), TECC represents a serious change in teacher education governance in Manitoba. Whereas the Minister cannot act unilaterally but only on the advice of TECC, the establishment of this "advisory" committee nevertheless marked a significant increase in government control ostensibly allied with the profession, and an equally significant decrease in institutional governance.

Two subsequent changes to teacher education certification requirements demonstrate the challenge of government control to institutional governance in Manitoba. The 2005 revisions to new teacher certification requirements for the early and middle years and a broadening of acceptable teachable subjects came about in response to university pressures and consultation with the profession. But, significantly, the government implemented these changes at the behest of TECC. Universities are now part of the process, not the decision-makers. In 2008, the government announced new Ministerial requirements for Special Education / Diversity and Aboriginal Education. Effective September 2009, all teacher education programs must contain a minimum of six credit hours of required Special Education / Diversity coursework and three credit hours of required Aboriginal Education coursework. Universities have to inform the government of how it would comply with these new requirements; the government, in turn, exercises its prerogative to approve or disapprove what was proposed. Thus, while institutional governance may still be alive in Manitoba teacher education, its actual powers have been seriously curtailed. Indeed, the imposition of the 2008 new Ministerial requirements for Special Education / Diversity and Aboriginal Education (which included conversations with course instructors about the specificity of content in the Aboriginal Education course) demonstrated the level of intervention to which the government was prepared to go as it involved itself in program and curriculum matters.

Thus, Manitoba is an example of how a provincial context that, historically and culturally, has been committed to institutional governance is being re-fashioned by macro-political pressures that have forged a government-controlled alliance between the profession and policy makers. The common feature across the provinces is the macro-political pressure that is impacting teacher education governance. In British Columbia and Ontario, these pressures have led to the establishment of professional self-regulation.

## Professional Governance:
## The Colleges of Teachers in British Columbia and Ontario

Professional self-regulatory bodies[5] have two broad purposes: (1) to regulate the profession of teaching by maintaining and improving the standards of professional conduct among teachers, in the interests of the public, and (2) to ensure that all members of the profession, including those joining it, meet professional standards that ensure the quality of learning for students. This second purpose gives the professional bodies a role to play in the governance

---

[5] The first professional regulatory body for teaching was established in 1965 in Scotland, the General Teaching Council of Scotland (GTCS). British Columbia, Canada, followed this lead in 1987 passing legislation to establish the BC College of Teachers (BCCT). In 1995, Ontario followed BC's example and passed legislation establishing the Ontario College of Teachers (OCT). Hence, two Canadian provinces have professional regulatory bodies in teaching. Others followed in 1998 in England (General Teaching Council), Wales (General Teaching Council of Wales), and Northern Ireland (General Teaching Council of Northern Ireland), and most recently, this decade has seen the establishment of professional bodies in Australia in Queensland (Queensland College of Teachers), Victoria (Victoria Institute of Teaching), New South Wales (New South Wales Institute of Teachers), and Western Australia (Professional Teaching Council of Western Australia).

of teacher education. Two of the most senior professional self-regulatory bodies involved in the governance of teacher education are found in British Columbia and Ontario.

The British Columbia College of Teachers (BCCT) and the Ontario College of Teachers (OCT) were established in 1988 and 1996, respectively. Each has a Council consisting of a majority of members elected from among the ranks of the teaching profession, with a minority representing the public who are appointed by the government. BCCT has a Council of 20 members, 12 are elected teachers and eight are appointed members. OCT has a Council of 37 members, 23 are elected teachers and 14 are appointed members. On both the BCCT and OCT councils, one of the appointed members represents the teacher education programs.

From its inception in 1988 until 2004, professional governance of teacher education in BC took on the form of a consultative approach to program approval when reviewing teacher education arrangements in the province. Two court decisions in 2001, however, brought about a fundamental change. First, the Supreme Court of Canada Decision—*Trinity Western University versus BCCT*—dismissed the BC College of Teachers' appeal of the Court of Appeal of British Columbia decision. The Court of Appeal of British Columbia decision had confirmed the order to the College to approve the Trinity Western University teacher education program and the conditions recommended by the BCCT's Teacher Education Programs Committee in 1996. Consequently, BCCT began the process of working with Trinity Western University to implement the court-ordered approval of their teacher education program. Second, the British Columbia Supreme Court Decision—*University of British Columbia versus the BC College of Teachers*—handed down a ruling on the judicial review application by the University of British Columbia at the decision by the BC College of Teachers to deny approval of the revised teacher education program at the University of British Columbia. The Court ruled that the college had exceeded its jurisdiction in establishing some of the conditions under which the council indicated it was prepared to approve the proposal from the University of British Columbia. The Court referred the matter back for re-consideration.

As a consequence of these two momentous Court decisions, BCCT undertook to co-construct with the Association of British Columbia Deans of Education (ABCDE) a Letter of Understanding that would govern how graduates from the eight existing teacher education programs in the province would be certified by BCCT. In 2004 this agreement was concluded. These programs must ensure that their graduates meet the Standards for the Education, Competence and Professional Conduct of Educators in BC. This historic agreement between the Association of BC Deans of Education and the college, signed on June 18, 2004, committed the two parties to work collaboratively to prepare and certify only those who meet the standards.

In 1995, the Ontario Royal Commission on Learning, "For the Love of Learning," recommended the establishment of a College of Teachers that would have authority for teaching standards, as well as for accreditation of teacher education programs, and for setting standards of professional development. Consequently, the Ontario College of Teachers Act in 1996 set up the college and also gave it responsibility for the accreditation of preservice teacher education. Each review includes an examination of the program to determine if it reflects such aspects as current Ontario curriculum plus relevant legislation and government policy related to curriculum, including the college's Standards of Practice for the Teaching Profession and the Ethical Standards for the Teaching Profession.

One of the ironies of the period in which BCCT and OCT were established is that the shift toward professional control through the articulation of standards was born in a policy context of deregulation. Moreover, professional governance can come into conflict with some of the values deemed central to a university in a manner that also affects the politics and power sharing that exists within and between universities and society. Currently in Ontario, OCT and the Ontario Deans of Education (OADE) are in dialogue about how they can "dance" (Grimmett & Echols, 2006) together regarding the accreditation of teacher education programs. In BC, BCCT and ABCDE are working hard to establish the conditions that can satisfy the professional body's need for accountability and the universities' need for institutional autonomy over program processes. These attempts at collaboration are not easy but appear to be an avenue that will likely provide for the continued exercise of professional expertise and judgment.

## Conclusion

Faced with a forced choice between external political interference and professional governance as the venue for crafting a compelling vision for teacher education, my argument is that the latter represents the better course of action. However, moving teacher education forward under professional governance is also problematic because professional self-regulatory bodies inherit their raison d'être from the neo-liberalist policy context. Their power is not their own; it is delegated to them by governments, and the potential is always there for so-called independent professional bodies to become the means whereby government directives are made more palatable. The public is also beginning to lose faith in such bodies to safeguard the public trust because they are perceived as working in their own institutional interest by fostering bureaucratic expansionism (Grimmett, 2008). Thus, they have become subject to similar pressure faced by universities in the 1990s.

If the governance of teacher education in Canada is to differ from the direct political control currently in force in the United States and England, then we need to find ways of forging a distinct approach. We must ensure that governance serves the public good by protecting those at the action level from unwarranted political intrusion, thereby enabling them to demonstrate the power of pedagogical knowing for student learning.

# RESPONSE

## Carolyn M. Shields

Peter Grimmett, in focusing on the complexities of teacher education in Canada, states that conducting teacher education in university settings in Canada is not "straightforward." And to be sure, the same is true in the United States and many other developed countries that have adopted forms of neo-liberal governance. At the end of his excellent discussion, he debates the relative merits of "external political interference" and "professional governance" and comes down on the side of the latter—a decision I will return to shortly.

During his discussion, he comes to a number of observations and conclusions that are similar to my own, despite the differences in context. For example, he identifies a diminishing role for universities in knowledge formation and cultural production. In fact, I might go farther, and ask whether, at present, any institution or governing body attends to those functions in the current governance contexts of either the United States or Canada. Peter also raises the related question of who attends to the public good in this era of individualism and competition, stating that, in the past, professionalism took on this responsibility. Again, there is no question that conversation about and concern for the public good have been almost totally overshadowed by an emphasis on education as a private good. Education, we are often told, assures individual career advancement, increased lifetime earnings, and better heath, welfare, and even happiness. Rarely is there discussion of education's role in promoting an educated citizenry and a civil society.

I take issue with Peter's conclusion that professional governance (as he describes it for Ontario and British Columbia, for example) will be a more viable means of protecting knowledge formation, cultural production, or the public good than legislated federal or state standards (which he identifies as "political interference"). Instead, what I have tried to demonstrate in my brief overview of the complex layers of governance of American education is that neither approach bodes well for equity, excellence, or democratic society. Despite my argument that higher standards are essential and that more equitable systems of local control are imperative, I believe that the answer lies beyond governance systems all together. We must look to the moral imperatives of treating all students with absolute regard, rejecting deficit thinking and pathologizing practices, and begin to expect excellence and high standards of achievement for all. The answer does not come from institutions or structures but from the hearts and minds of caring, critical, and dedicated educators, and hence, from a thorough revision of the mission, values, and pedagogies of professional education programs. It is to that end that teacher and professional education must refocus its attention, for I know of no other forum for effecting a more equitable and excellent education for all children.

## We invite the reader to consider the following questions:

1. What kinds of policies are needed to direct the governance of American education toward fostering equality and equity for all students? On what guiding principles would such policies be based?

2. How is the governance of the K–12 education system connected with the governance of teacher education? What needs to happen in the education of teachers to ensure that beginning practitioners see teaching as contributing to the public good of an equitable education? How can a new political mind-set be developed to counter neo-liberalist tendencies that undervalue equity in education?

3. If one way to create more equitable and excellent education is to raise minimum standards, what should they be, and who should make those decisions?

4. If another way to improve education is through professional education programs for teachers and leaders, then what should be their core values, content, and pedagogies—and again, whose voices should be heard as decisions are made?

# THEME 2

# Exploring the Landscape of Teacher Education

CONTRIBUTING AUTHORS

Ruth Kane

Thomas Falkenberg

# The Teacher Education Landscape of My Imagining

*Ruth Kane*

When seeking to identify the kinds of learning and teacher education practices that would support beginning teachers in facing the challenges of the changing world, I am driven to look both to the past and to the future. In this essay I will attempt to define and address guiding questions by mapping the landscape of teacher education as I know it and as I would wish it to be. I take as my starting point reflections of times across my career as a teacher educator when others' comments have magnified how teacher education is perceived by those inside and outside universities. These perceptions are far from positive and although I believe them to be misconceptions, I do agree that as teacher educators we have often failed to serve as well as we might. I will then draw on the inspirational work of three colleagues in teacher education to demonstrate that there are alternative paths for teacher education to follow to prepare beginning teachers who are better able to serve the children and young people of the future.

## Reflections

*The genesis of my doctoral studies began in a university in Australia in 1993 when student teachers repeatedly returned from their practicum experience with stories of classroom teachers and principals who openly ridiculed the substance of the teacher education program—claiming it was of little real value when navigating a curriculum in a classroom and a school. The teacher education program was reportedly described as "merely a necessary hurdle for registration," "a waste of time," and programs were claimed to be "largely irrelevant and populated by professors who have lost touch with the classroom and with what real teaching is all about." I received my doctorate, which culminated in a thesis focused on an innovative approach to teacher education, and my mother, proud as she was of my achievement, commented, "But you are not a real doctor, are you? You cannot help people who are sick, you train teachers." Move ahead five years and I find myself leading the introduction to a teacher education program in a leading research university in New Zealand that had previously only taught the study of education, leaving the preparation of teachers to a local teachers college. At a daylong retreat for professors and senior administration in the Division of Humanities, a leading professor lamented: "Otago University doing teacher education—what next? Will we be introducing a degree in knitting?" After presenting my proposal for a two-year teacher education program, a senior professor of History questioned why a history honours graduate who has clearly demonstrated an excellent knowledge of her discipline, should be required to undertake teacher education in any form. He argued that "such a graduate should be allowed to be a teacher without the proposed two years' teacher education, for she is surely well qualified to do so." Move on another five years and I find myself Director of Teacher Education in a Canadian university. I am seeking to initiate change in a teacher education program to require student teachers to actively inquire into their own development as teachers and examine the assumptions and values underpinning their own and others' practices. I am told by a senior colleague, "You are wasting your time; you should focus instead on preparing your file for tenure. You need to learn that change is not appreciated by your colleagues, they have to focus on their research and publications."*

Within such comments lie some of the fundamental challenges of teacher education. First, school teachers repeatedly report that teacher education is not relevant and unhelpful. Second, teaching is generally perceived as familiar, lacking in status, and, to be blunt, so very ordinary. Third, even within higher education, teacher education is held in extremely low regard academically as "there is not much more to teaching than knowing the subject matter that children should learn" (Darling-Hammond & Baratz-Snowden, 2005). And fourth, within education faculties there are explicit pressures to focus on one's own advancement in the academy, and the closer one is associated with teachers and schools, the lower one's status; and the lower one's status, the fewer resources are available to support one's research and practice (Zeichner, 1995, 2005).

Teacher education, and the related study of teaching and learning to teach, does not have an especially salubrious history within universities. The study of teaching and teacher education have been neglected by university management, patently ignored and openly ridiculed by faculty from other disciplines, and variously avoided by professors within faculties of education. For those of us who have a passion for and take intellectual and professional challenge in the preparation of teachers and the study of teaching and teacher education practice, this historical neglect is at the least confounding and frustrating and at worst calls into question our work with student teachers and, for many, our scholarship. So what is it about this "bizarre, complex and misunderstood world of teacher education" (Kincheloe, 2004, p. 1) that leads to such confusion, derision, and explicit contempt?

Teacher education, while perceived by most to be quite straightforward, is messy, unpredictable, loaded with inconsistencies, and enormously complex. Some inconsistencies arise due to the misconceptions of those entering teacher education; others emanate from the teacher educators themselves. It is little wonder that students entering teacher education programs take for granted what teaching is all about. They have spent 12 or more years in school classrooms observing teachers at work and have formed their own conceptions of what it means to be a teacher. But as students, they were observers of teaching practice, unable to intuit the pedagogical principles, the personal beliefs, the on-the-spot thinking, or the underlying assumptions guiding the observable practice (Ethell & McMeniman, 2000). Unlike students entering other professional programs such as medicine and law, student teachers come armed with personal beliefs, conceptions, and most importantly experience of having been taught, and this "over familiarity of the teaching profession is a significant contradiction affecting those learning to teach" (Britzman, 2003, p. 27).

The lot of the teacher educator is no less demanding and ambiguous than is the lot of the student teacher. Some teacher educators are recruited from the field as expert teachers, and there is often an assumption (misguided) that expertise in teaching will transfer seamlessly into their new role as teaching educator (Kane, 2007; Loughran, 2006; Murray & Male, 2005; Zeichner, 2005). Others may have come through the academic study of educational foundations, for example, psychology, sociology, or subject-based disciplines such as mathematics or history. There are also the school-based associate teachers, who work with student teachers during practicum. These teachers are typically "enculturated by a technically rational teacher education and teaching workplace" (Kincheloe, 2004). Add to this mix the doctoral students and adjunct staff recruited to supervise practicum and teach professional inquiry and professional practice courses. These members of the teacher education community often have little connection to the program, may have little if any teaching experience, have limited knowledge of teacher education research, and a negligible voice or authority in the institution (Zeichner, 2005). The teacher education community comprises practitioners, researchers, graduate students, and scholars whose agendas may at first glance appear difficult to reconcile.

National and international publications signal that teacher educators are purposefully responding to the escalating importance of "issues related to teacher quality and quality teacher education" (Cochran-Smith & Zeichner, 2005, p. vii). Yet, in spite of the growing consensus that teachers matter, there is continued uncertainty as to "how and why they matter or how they should be recruited, prepared, and retained in teaching" (p. 1). Teacher educators operate in contexts that to date have been unable or unwilling to articulate a pedagogical model that can at least be used as the basis for common discourse and dialogue. Yet, in the last decade, international publications by leading teacher educators have given great cause for hope within teacher education. I will mention just three of these works as a way of signalling that there is huge potential for us to reconceptualize teacher education so that we prepare teachers for how schools could be rather than for how schools are.

From the Netherlands, Fred Korthagen (2001) proposes the *Pedagogy of Realistic Teacher Education* wherein students' experiences and responses to those experiences are the starting point of learning to teach, rather than objective theories on learning and teaching from the literature. Korthagen argues that it is the development of *phronesis* (perceptual knowledge) rather than *episteme* (science understanding or conceptual knowledge) that is key for teacher education as this knowledge leads to teachers who understand themselves as teachers rather than teachers who know a lot about teaching. The focus is on enabling student teachers to experience, make meaning, and interpret classroom practice and through this process to examine their own developing identities as teachers and how these identities impact on their pedagogy.

From the U.S.A., Joe Kincheloe wanted universities to "produce rigorously educated teachers with an awareness of the complexities of educational practice and an understanding of and commitment to a socially just, democratic notion of schooling" (2004, p. 24). Kincheloe proposes a critical complex vision of teacher education that recognises "different types of knowledges of education, including but not limited to empirical, experiential, normative, critical, ontological, and reflective-synthetic domains" (p. 27). In this vision, teaching constitutes knowledge (Munby & Russell, 1994) and teaching is first and foremost epistemological (Kincheloe, 2004).

Australian John Loughran's *Developing a Pedagogy of Teacher Education* confronts head on the hitherto absence of such a pedagogy by articulating, describing, and examining the complex "relationship between teaching and learning in the programs and practices of learning *and* teaching about teaching" (2006, p. 3). Pivotal to developing a pedagogy of teacher education, Loughran argues, is understanding the interdependent worlds of "teaching about teaching and learning about teaching" (p. 174). Expanding on the work of Russell (1997), Korthagen (2001), Hoban (2005) and others in the Self Study of Teaching and Teacher Education community, Loughran further argues that:

> Being part of the experience matters in a pedagogy of teacher education because it is about enacting practices that are sensitive and responsive to the cognitive and affective needs, issues and concerns in teaching and learning about teaching. (2006, p. 175)

Teacher education in this view requires both student teachers and teacher educators to carefully examine their own practices and the impact of such practices on our ongoing learning about teaching.

Each of the aforementioned scholars brings new conceptions of teacher education into focus by proposing alternative views of knowledge and practice related to teacher education. For each, reflection on and synthesis of different ways of knowing and practicing are essential elements. The student teacher's development of a sense of self as teacher is also fundamental. Teacher education has shifted from the technical-rational view of teaching to one where the student teacher's development goes well beyond simply acquiring knowledge, skills, and dispositions to negotiate a class.

The structures of teacher education programs internationally share similar elements. Most include the study of the purpose and goals of education and how children learn (educational foundations), courses in curriculum and pedagogy (what and how to teach), and school-based practicum (teaching practice). However, in spite of these structural similarities, there is limited agreement on a knowledge base or a pedagogy of teacher education. To date we have been tinkering at the edges of teacher education, making cosmetic changes within the restrictive policies and regulations that govern degrees and professors' workloads and within cultures that do not foster "collaborative work on the question of how to improve the pedagogy of teacher education" (Korthagen, 2001, p. 8). To meet the goals articulated by Korthagen (2001), Kincheloe (2004), Loughran (2006), and Russell and Loughran (2007), to name but a few, we need to break free of the old ways of thinking about teacher education. This would require a fundamental shift in how teacher educators view themselves and their role in the preparation of teachers.

As teacher educators we are charged with preparing teaching for the 21st century. There is no doubt that we need to graduate new teachers who are able to serve well the children and young people of the future.

> Today's student teachers will work in classrooms for the next 40 years and will work with children who themselves will influence and participate in society through 2070 and beyond (Braslavsky, 2001).

This is an awesome challenge and one that we should not take lightly.

While I believe we can predict little about the school curricula of the coming decades, we can be sure of one thing—our classrooms will become more diverse in terms of ethnicity, linguistic background, culture, class, spiritual beliefs, and abilities. So far this century is proving to be a challenging period in which, in the face of increasing diversity and associated tensions locally and globally, education is becoming more prescribed and the language of "common curriculum," "standards," "quality," and "accountability" reverberate through school staff rooms, relegating teachers to technicians delivering a mandated curriculum developed by others and suited only to some. The system is responding in ways that will ensure that diversity leads to disadvantage and unequal access and outcomes. The danger lies in teacher education not challenging such ineffective policies and practices and graduating new teachers who have known no better way to teach. We need to move beyond thinking of teacher education in terms of preparing teachers for today's schools and look toward imagining how we can prepare teachers for schools that could be.

Each teacher education community is socially, culturally, and politically situated within a particular context that comprises professors, students, and local school partners. In addition, there are Ministry of Education and/or accreditation requirements and university policies and procedures that govern the design and conduct of degree programs. Setting these aside for now, let us begin with the partners—professors, students, and teachers. While it may well be naïve, I would like to propose a landscape of teacher education that assumes support from colleagues and a structural context that welcomes and supports change. I am imagining a landscape that begins not with mapping the visible structure and content, the number of courses or credits, but with the essence of the program's intentions: its underlying values and theoretical assumptions. I begin by asking what values, beliefs, and assumptions are critical to teacher education?

The conceptual framework of a qualification articulates clearly and coherently the assumptions, beliefs, values, ethics, and understandings that are of particular importance to that teacher education community. It makes explicit the underlying conceptions of, for example, education, teaching, learning, schooling, and learning to teach. The collaborative development of a conceptual framework requires the community of teacher educators to respect and consider each other's knowledge and expertise, to engage in purposeful dialogue, to question what is taken for granted, and together to take a position, to avoid neutrality and dare to articulate what teacher education means to them. Paulo Freire challenged "those who dare to teach" to demonstrate a commitment to freedom and social justice or risk that their teaching would become meaningless (1998, p.4).

The teacher education landscape of my imagining would be one grounded in a commitment to

- freedom and social justice through inclusionary education,
- examining the power of education in a sustainable global world,
- teaching and learning about teaching through critical reflection and analysis of experiences of self and others,
- supporting student teachers in their development as critical educators.

While such ethics are easy to articulate as independent elements, in practice they would be represented by an interdependent matrix from which key questions are generated that challenge teacher educators and guide our work with student teachers. As argued by each of the aforementioned scholars, it is not good enough for us to promote such ideals for our student teachers—these are commitments that we as teacher educators must sincerely adopt and emulate in all aspects of our work.

Commitment to inclusionary education may be approached in different ways within teacher education programs, but teacher educators "must have a *vision* of teaching and learning in a diverse society," and this vision must infuse the teacher education curriculum (Villegas & Lucas, 2002, p. 20, emphasis added). To ensure that students from marginalized groups are fully included, the past and current exclusionary practices that prevent children and young people from full participation must be highlighted and targeted so that the "wider socio-political origins of discrimination and oppression in schools and communities" can be understood and thus overcome (Booth & Ainscow, 1998). An underlying commitment to inclusionary education would necessarily employ Kincheloe's knowledges of education (2004) so as to achieve a fuller understanding of how inclusion operates in a teaching (and teacher education) context.

To develop global perspectives of education, student teachers need opportunities to critique how "historical forces have shaped the purposes of schooling" and focus on the "political and power-related aspects of teacher education and teaching" (Kincheloe, 2004, p. 35). Student teachers must develop an understanding of how education is situated within the wider social and political contexts, locally and internationally, and be able to analyse how and why the education system has evolved as it is. First, though, teacher educators must develop a shared vision and global perspective for education and teacher education. If we are, as I am sure is the case, committed to preparing quality teachers for democratic classrooms, then we would do well to attend to Freire's tenet that "The more people become themselves, the better the democracy" (Horton & Freire, 1990).

It seems to me that most teacher education programs today advocate a commitment to reflective practice and yet the degree to which this is achieved in our graduates is questionable. It is over 100 years since Dewey (1974) called out the need for student teachers to practice reflective inquiry. Van Manen (1977) elaborated on Dewey's notion of reflection and Schön (1987) directed attention to the practitioner's ability to engage in "reflection-in-action" and "reflection-on-action." In a commitment to critical reflection on practice, I am further informed by the realistic approach to teacher education (Korthagen, 2001) wherein the practice of the student teacher is the starting point for the examination of the perceptual knowledge embedded in and emerging from practice. Korthagen's (2001) model (ALACT) is a spiral process of reflection comprising five phases that locates reflection at the centre of the pedagogy of teacher education. In the teacher education landscape of my imagining, it would be the teacher educators who would first engage in and articulate their "seeing inside of teaching" (Loughran, 2006). In teaching teachers we need to ensure that what we ask of student teachers we ourselves have the capacity and commitment to also practice.

The final commitment within the teacher education landscape of my imagining would be to place the student teacher's developing professional knowledge of self as teacher at the centre of the learning-to-teach process. In so doing I believe we need to begin with the student teachers' preconceptions of teaching. Working from how student teachers understand teaching and learning and learning to teach, teacher educators must provide opportunities for alternative interpretations by posing critical questions that encourage student teachers to examine their preconceptions and the forces and cultural knowledges that have impacted their understandings.

One of the critical features of strong teacher education programs is that they are "particularly well integrated and coherent: they have integrated clinical work with coursework so that it reinforces and reflects key ideas and both aspects of the program build towards a deeper understanding of teaching and learning" (Darling-Hammond et al., 2005, p. 390). Coherent teacher education programs are grounded in a set of big ideas that are continually revised as both faculty and school-based teacher educators work toward a shared vision of teaching and learning.

In presenting the teacher education landscape of my imagining, I am wilfully setting aside those institutional policies that may constrain the design. I would argue that teacher education is unique in the university. It operates in a context of uncertainty, and for the teacher educator that which is taught (teaching) is not only that which is done (teaching) but also for many of us is that which is the focus of our research (teaching). This is not the case for other professional disciplines, such as medicine and law. Typically, the content that is taught and is the focus of research, be it propositional or procedural in nature, can be separated from the practice of teaching. In no discipline other than teacher education is the content and the process of teaching and researching that content so entangled. (Ham & Kane, 2004) From this unique position, I advocate that we first articulate the underlying foundations of a teacher education program, which must be based on principles that are ethically grounded and defendable. From thence we can develop the structures, courses, and credits and, if necessary, negotiate the policies and regulations. In this way we can create a teacher education landscape worthy of serving the children and young people of the future.

# RESPONSE

## Thomas Falkenberg

In my brief response, I would like to highlight a point that Ruth raises, a point that is also visible in her description of the landscape of teacher education, a point that deserves to be at the forefront of our attention to teacher education, and a point that cannot be stressed enough: "teacher education, while perceived by most to be quite straightforward, is messy, unpredictable, loaded with inconsistencies and enormously complex." I would like to discuss two such "messy" aspects by drawing from Ruth's essay, which presents those aspects so nicely.

First, as Ruth suggests, we should "prepare teachers for how schools could be rather than for how schools are." But, as Ruth also suggests—following Korthagen—we might find great value in making school experiences the starting point for learning to teach, and that generally means experiences in schools *as they are*. Knowing from the literature how important field experiences are considered by teacher candidates—often in stark contrast to their university courses experience—Korthagen's spiral model of reflective practice cannot avoid being entangled in the pedagogical tension between "ought" and "is": How schools *are* shapes teacher candidates' interpretative framework for their experiences ("apprenticeship of observation") and, thus, their response to any suggestions of how schools *ought* to be. And any vision of how schools *ought* to be faces the perceived "constraints of reality" that are filtered through the perception of how schools *are*. When following Ruth's idea of "posing critical questions that encourage student teachers to examine their preconceptions, and the forces and cultural knowledges that have impacted their understandings," we need to keep in mind that the teacher candidates' interpretative framework will determine their self-examination.

Second, Ruth suggests a parallel endeavour for teacher candidates and teacher educators to undertake: "teaching and learning about teaching through critical reflection and analysis of experiences of self and others." She suggests that teacher candidates are helped to understand their "preconceptions of teaching" by considering critical questions that challenge the "personal beliefs, conceptions and most importantly experience of teaching" that they bring into teacher education programs. She also suggests that "what we [the teacher educators] ask of the student teachers we ourselves have the capacity and commitment to practice." While this might sound straightforward, the "messiness," "inconsistencies," and "enormous complexities" all quickly rise to the surface when we dig a little bit deeper: The critical questions posed by teacher educators to teacher candidates are based in teacher educators' understandings of such alternative interpretations of teacher candidates' experiences. Those understandings of teacher candidates' experiences are linked to teacher educators' engagement with their own experiences. Who is posing critical questions to the teacher educators concerning their interpretive framework? And more importantly, if the process of engaging with one's own experiences as a teacher educator is to be seen as an ongoing process, then the basis upon which teacher educators provide teacher candidates with alternative interpretations of their experiences is always "temporary" and "fluid." These endeavours get even "messier" if one advocates the critical standard of coherency for strong teacher education programs, as Ruth does, and suggests that teacher educators need to "develop a shared vision and global perspective for education and teacher education." With the rich experiences and perspectives represented in a faculty of teacher educators, how much of a shared vision can we expect, and how fragile will that vision be?

# Starting with the End in Mind

## Ethics-of-Care-Based Teacher Education

*Thomas Falkenberg*

### Introduction

My concern lies with teacher education, but as Goodlad (1990, p. 3)—and probably many before him—points out: "The education of teachers must be driven by a clear and careful conception of the educating we expect our schools to do." It is probably here where it becomes clear that the *that* and *how* of teacher education is normative at its very core: What type of educating do we expect our schools to do? The central task of teacher education programs, then, is to prepare teacher candidates for this type of educating. In this essay I argue that such teacher preparation is best done by helping teacher candidates develop as ethics-of-care-based agents.

### Teaching as a Moral Enterprise

Teaching is inherently moral because of its intent and its effect. Teaching, as Fenstermacher (1990, p. 133) points out, "is, quite centrally, human action undertaken in regard to other human beings"; when we teach, we are concerned about the development, the learning, and the betterment of our students. But teaching is also inherently moral because of the effect it may have on students' morality; when we ask students to work together with other students, when we select and apply punitive consequences for disapproved student behaviour, or when we teach about democratic citizenship, we may have considerable impact on our students' social orientation, their attitude toward learning, or their outlook on life. Meaningful teaching for intellectual development—which is so central in our academic curricula—should be *moral* in its effect, because we should want our students, in the words of John Dewey (1975), to acquire intellectual ideas "in such a vital way that they become *moving* ideas, motive-forces in the guidance of conduct" (p. 2), and what could be more moral than such moving ideas?

From this perspective then, teacher education should prepare candidates for teaching as a moral enterprise.[1] But to derive anything programmatic from this imperative, the view of teaching as a moral enterprise must be embedded in a theory of morality, which would provide us with a more explicit normative and conceptual framework for considering the world around and within us. To delineate our theory of morality, we would need clear definitions for conceptual terms such as "moral purpose," "moral understanding," "norms," "expectations," "needs," and so on.

As I have argued elsewhere (Falkenberg, in press), any such theory of morality makes assumptions about what I call "the human condition," which is a net of assumptions about the basic conditions under which we humans live our lives. Such assumptions need and should be only *partially* philosophical in nature; the human sciences, including biology, psychology, sociology, and the cognitive sciences, have a lot to tell us about the human condition. Rooted in the traditions of existentialism, hermeneutic perspectivism, and socio-constructionism (Gadamer, 1989; Heidegger, 1962; Martin, Sugarman, & Thompson, 2003), the philosophical aspects of my perspective on the human condition see at the core of being human a concern for how we should live our life. Born into and by necessity participating in an already existing socio-cultural environment and equipped with developing memory and imagination, agency emerges in us and allows us to interact dynamically with our socio-cultural environment. This human agency is characterized by socio-culturally embedded self-determination, which allows us to be less constrained by instinct, habituation, and impulse than other living beings. But with self-determination, the existential question of how we *should* live our life becomes prominent in living our life.

This perspective on the human condition has two key implications for education. First, if at the core of the human condition is the existential question of how we should live our lives, then the general purpose of schooling must be to help students respond to this existential concern. The second implication concerns the normative character of this existential question. Teaching, I argued above, is inherently moral in purpose, because it is human action regarding other human beings. The perspective taken here on the hu-

---

[1] This claim is non-exclusive. I do not want to exclude or diminish other important preparation aspects in teacher education, such as preparing teacher candidates for particular subject-matter teaching, planning engaging learning activities, assessing student learning, and so on. What I do suggest, however, is that due to the inherently moral character of teaching, preparing teachers for teaching as a moral enterprise must be the overarching idea in teacher education, penetrating thinking about all aspects of preparation in teacher education programs.

man condition provides a more concrete view of the moral purpose of schooling: at its core, *the moral purpose of schooling* is to help students with their emerging existential concern for how they should live their lives.

If we take this moral purpose of schooling seriously, much of what is currently done in institutionalized education in Canada is questionable as an adequate response to students' existential concerns. For instance, artificially inflated expectations of more and more formal education force many youth and young adults to stay in school against their own and most likely against society's needs. On the other hand, what I would consider central to students' existential concerns is either not at all or only peripherally addressed; these concerns would include how to build and sustain relationships, live healthy, understand the role of spirituality in being human, deal with needs and desires, deal with leisure time, and deal with uncertainty and contradicting constraints.

I suggest *an ethic of care* as the theory of morality that should govern teaching as the moral enterprise of helping students respond to their existential concerns about how to live their lives.

## An Ethic of Care as the Theory of Morality for Teaching and Schooling

For about the last decade, caring and teacher-student relationships have been finding their way onto the list of central concerns in the professional education community in North America, as can be seen in their publications (see, for instance, *Building Classroom Relationships*, 2003; *Creating Caring Schools*, 2003; Deiro, 1996; Gootman, 2000). Much of this literature and the concerns connected with it, however, are quite distinct in key respects from the notion of ethics-of-care-based education that I am suggesting here. The central distinction is that the former is *not* grounded in the ethics of care as a moral theory; rather, no reference to an ethical framework is made and "caring" is meant in the general sense of "being respectful and considerate of others," or, as Lisa Goldstein quotes one teacher candidate: "A caring teacher has to have love, love, and more love for children" (2002, p. 74). In the following, I will focus on caring as a notion grounded in the ethics of care.

Although there are differences in detail among approaches to the ethics of care, it is safe to claim that the ethics of care as a theory of morality has three central features (Falkenberg, 2006): a relational ontology, a concern for human needs, and a subscription to particularism. Grounded in a Kantian liberal political philosophy, the enculturated view in Western societies is one in which the individual is seen as an autonomous moral being who rationally deliberates or reflects upon what is right and wrong to do in particular situations, based on moral principles of right and wrong or good and bad. In opposition to this view stands the view of humans as relational beings, whose very existence and well-being depend on the quality of their relationships to others. From this *ontological* principle of relational interdependence, Nel Noddings—probably the best-known proponent of the ethics of care—derives an *ethical* principle of relational responsibility:

> Contrary to Kant, who insisted that each person's moral perfection is his or her own project, we remain at least partly responsible for the moral development of each person we encounter. (2002, p. 15)

The ethics of care is a needs-and-response-based moral code at the core of which are—as this characterization suggests—our attention and response to human needs. In opposition to the widespread Kantian idea of principle-based moral deliberation (Kant, 1988; Kohlberg, 1987, ch. 7), the ethics of care subscribes to particularism, according to which situational particulars should be given preference over general principles in our moral deliberation.

From these three features, Noddings, in particular, postulates that an ethics of care should concern how we human beings build, sustain, and improve our caring relations with each other. Adopting this view of an ethic of care to define the moral foundation of teaching and the purpose of schooling as helping students with their existential concerns about how they should live their lives, I believe schooling should help students learn, practice, and experience building, sustaining, and improving caring relations.

Therefore, I suggest a particular view of an ethics-of-care-based agency. It is this agency that will guide our self-determination and our dynamic interaction with our socio-cultural environment. The notion of an ethics-of-care-based agency is not incompatible with the relational ontology underlying the ethics of care but is intended to conceptualize what it is that is in relationship.

At the core of my conceptualization of an ethics-of-care-based agency is the view of *caring as a lived moral practice*, a practice that has as its driving core the concern for human needs.[2] I see three agentic qualities required for caring as a lived moral practice. First, we need to cultivate the disposition to be emotionally and intelligently concerned about human needs. This disposition has attitudinal and skill-based components to make the ethics-of-care-based agent willing and able to be concerned about human needs in an ethics-of-care-based sense, namely, being concerned when facing human needs, being aware of human needs, and taking an inquiry stance that, in particular,

---

[2] I limit my considerations here to the domain of *human* needs.

has us constantly questioning our assumptions about the needs we subscribe to ourselves as well as others. Second, we need to have an imaginative world vision of a holistic life of care. It is such a vision that helps us balance our different, often incompatible, "care commitments." Third, we need to be effective (have an effect) as ethics-of-care-based agents in the sense that we are actually enacting caring as lived moral practice and not just cultivating the disposition for it.

Ethics-of-care-based education, then, has as its central purpose to help students develop (further) their ethics-of-care-based agency. Ethics-of-care-based education is moral education and as such requires in particular enculturating students into caring as a lived moral practice, which means students need to experience, practice, and reflect on caring as a lived moral practice. This can best be done, I suggest, in a culture that is created, maintained, and worked on by teachers who engage in caring as a lived moral practice themselves, which means teachers who exert a well-developed ethics-of-care-based agency. This, then, has implications for teacher education. I will now turn to these implications.

## Ethics-of-Care-Based Teacher Education

I quoted John Goodlad (1990, p. 3) above as stating that "the education of teachers must be driven by a clear and careful conception of the educating we expect our schools to do." In the previous section I have outlined a conception of such ethics-of-care-based education. Adopting Goodlad's perspective on the relationship between schooling and teacher education and considering what I said about the need for teachers to be well-developed agents for such an education, teacher education from this point of view, then, has the central task of helping teacher candidates with the development of their own ethics-of-care-based agency as it particularly concerns their work in schools. The focus in ethics-of-care-based teacher education, then, is on *being* a teacher rather than on learning to teach, on forming an ethics-of-care-based teacher *identity* rather than on knowledge and technical proficiency. This, of course, is more a statement of emphasis than of mutual exclusivity, since knowing how to teach can be a condition for being the teacher one likes and might need to be to address students' needs. For instance, being proficient in designing and implementing differentiated lessons can help a teacher address her concern for the competing needs of her students.

In the remainder of this section, I will illustrate a teacher education program that is guided by the concern for developing teacher candidates' ethics-of-care-based agency as it particularly concerns their work in schools. For illustrative purposes I will ignore program constraints of different types, among which are resources, traditions, certification, and incompatible views on teacher education within the faculty. For space reasons some features will be sketchier than others, and most of the justification of the features with respect to the theoretical framework outlined in this essay will have to be rather brief.

The program is grounded in the idea of ethics-of-care-based education as explicated above. Thus, it is guided by the idea of helping teacher candidates develop their ethics-of-care-based agency: developing the disposition to be emotionally and intelligently concerned about human needs, developing their imaginative world vision of a holistic life of care, and becoming effective as ethics-of-care-based agents. To that end, I suggested that it is important that teacher candidates experience, practice, and reflect upon caring as lived moral practice. The two-year program is not structured by individual courses in the usual sense. Rather, a small group of teacher educators takes on a cohort of students for the entire length of the program, jointly and alternately engaging the teacher candidates in a program curriculum whose components are coordinated and in tune with the overall objective of ethics-of-care-based teacher education. The focus on *being* more than *knowing*, for caring as a lived moral practice more than proficiency in teaching the program and its curriculum, requires a certain level of intimacy and trust among those in the program. Thus, the teacher education program and course structure needs to allow for a longer engagement between teacher educator and teacher candidates.[3]

Concern for the development of ethics-of-care-based agency in teacher candidates suggests a focus on teacher candidates as persons who come with particular needs that are framed by their hopes, beliefs, biases, and personal learning history. Thus, although the program curriculum is framed by the teacher educators' view of what it means to engage in such education, the actual form the curriculum takes in the program is co-constructed by the teacher educators and the teacher candidates through their perceived and expressed needs as teacher candidates.

Teacher candidates' life history (Carter & Doyle, 1996) is a central source for understanding individual teacher candidates' particular needs as aspiring teachers, as is, of course, the program's view of the teaching the schools are expected to do. The scholarship of personal history studies in teacher education suggests that teacher candidates use their own experiences as students (life history) "as prototypical and generalizable for interpreting

---

[3] Under the term "continuity of people" Noddings makes the same case for the teacher-student relationship in schools (Noddings, 1992, p. 68–69).

and making decisions about the teaching practices they encounter in courses and field experiences" (Carter & Doyle, 1996, p. 127). Understanding teacher candidates' "autobiographical self" (Damasio, 1999), therefore, is an important element in understanding teacher candidates' needs as learners. Drawing on arguments made in Carter and Doyle (1996) and Doyle and Carter (2003) for a contextualized biographical narration of experience as a way of developing a knowledge base for teaching, the starting point for the negotiated program curriculum is the critical autobiographical writing that teacher candidates are asked to do, reflecting on their history as learners and their developed understanding of what teaching is.[4] From this, a differentiated curriculum for teacher candidates will result.[5] Currently, teacher education programs are differentiated by grade-level (for instance, elementary, secondary) and subject matter needs (for high school preparation). In the program here described, however, the differentiation is *within* the joint cohort and can mean, for instance, different types of assignments and readings and different levels and forms of involvement with students in schools.

The learning and teaching of a subject matter are guided in the program by the notion of caring for ideas (Noddings, 1992, ch. 11), a central element of the educational response to students' existential concerns. For instance, the question of how mathematics as a human activity can contribute to addressing people's existential concerns for how they should live their lives and for living a holistic life of care would be key to teacher candidates' learning to teach mathematics.

To address teacher candidates' imaginative world vision of a holistic life of care, the program introduces teacher candidates to philosophy as an educational practice (Hadot, 1995; Nozick, 1989). The object of this practice is the understanding of a community and life of care. Burbules and Warnick (2006) provide ten specific methods of philosophical inquiry that form the backbone of teacher candidates' inquiry into questions such as "What does it mean to live a life grounded in an ethic of care?," "What societal conditions promote or impede a communal life of care?," and "What are human needs?"

To help teacher candidates cultivate an emotionally and intelligently concerned disposition toward human needs along with the attitudinal and skill-based components of that disposition, the "inner life of the educator" (Palmer, 1998; Cohen, 2006) must be a central part of the curriculum. One

---

[4] The "critical" qualifier refers to Britzman's (1991) emphasis of "the importance of teachers examining their life stories within a larger historical frame" (Carter & Doyle, 1996, p. 128).

[5] Differentiation has always been part of curricular thinking from an ethics-of-care-based perspective (see, for instance, Noddings, 1992, pp. 151–159).

aspect of this "inner life" concerns questions about what moves us in particular situations to act or respond in particular ways and to notice alternative possibilities and develop in-the-moment sensitivities that help us be more concerned and responsive to human needs. John Mason (2002) suggested a "Discipline of Noticing" that could serve as a guide for developing such attitudinal and skill-based components of caring as a lived moral practice. The "Discipline of Noticing" provides for a rigorous and systematic regime of inquiring into one's (life) practices with the purpose of changing those in a desirable direction. The program here described makes use of this discipline of noticing by asking teacher candidates to keep an account of their engagements with their students and their learning in the program. They then are guided to look for and identify common threads, themes, and issues in those accounts. Drawing on understandings of living a life of care from the philosophical practices described above, situations of particular types are identified by teacher candidates as situations in which they want to respond differently; for instance, one teacher candidate might notice that she always responds with anger first and foremost when a student has not completed his or her homework assignment. Labelling those types of situations and vividly imagining oneself acting differently can help teacher candidates to (a) notice those situations better in-the-moment, (b) notice more alternatives for acting in those situations, and (c) develop stronger inclinations to act differently in those situations. Practicing such noticing, then, can eventually lead to a more habitual feeling and acting in the desired way; for instance, the teacher candidate might instead feel more concerned and inquire about the reasons a student has not completed her homework.

Traditionally in Canada, although this is slowly changing, the academic university courses and the school-based practica are separated by space, time, and personnel. The envisioned teacher education program transcends this separation by integrating university classes, concrete classroom experiences, and practica. At least partially, university classes are now being taught in schools, where the teacher candidates' classroom experiences are infused with reflections on teacher educators and teacher candidates' ethics-of-care-based engagement, and where classes about this approach to education are infused with concrete experiences of the complexity of teaching and caring relationships. The practicum, then, is designed as an extension of this form of teaching and learning engagement, with an ongoing practicum seminar held twice a week in the respective practicum school with a collaborating classroom teacher and a teacher educator.[6] Such integration provides opportunities for teacher candidates in the program to develop caring as a lived moral practice by being effective (having an effect as) ethics-of-care-based agents and by developing their disposition to be emotionally and intelligently concerned about human needs through their engagement with students and their supported reflections upon that engagement. All aspects of teaching practice, such as subject-matter teaching, assessment, and classroom management, are framed through this lens of ethics-of-care-based education.

Teacher candidates are not merely asked to practice and reflect upon caring as a lived moral practice but also to experience and be enculturated into caring as a lived moral practice. It is here in particular where the "ethics-of-care-based quality" of the teacher educators (and that includes the collaborating practicum teachers) themselves is of great importance. Because of their role in the design and practice of the program, teacher educators are key to creating, sustaining, and modifying the cultural experiences of teacher candidates. For that reason, weekly meetings are set up for smaller groups of teacher educators to engage in a communal self-study of their teaching and living practice, focusing on the development of their ethics-of-care-based agency. Particular aspects of practice, such as one's teaching in the program or one's engagement with students and colleagues, are framed as matters of enacted ethics-of-care-based agency.[7] The practices of helping teacher candidates develop their ethics-of-care-based agency suggested above, such as autobiographical writing, seeing one's teaching practice and engagement with others through an ethics-of-care-based lens, philosophizing about life matters, and the discipline of noticing, are all used in the communal self-study. Paraphrasing Goodlad's quote introducing this section, the (self) education of teacher educators must be driven by clear and careful conceptions of the educating they expect themselves to do.

## Conclusion

Teacher education program considerations need to start with the program's end in mind, and the end, in Goodlad's words, is the educating we expect our schools to do. In this essay I have conceptualized one such end — ethics-

---

[6] The school-university partnership envisioned here is not unlike the one found in professional development schools (see, for instance, Darling-Hammond, 2005).

[7] There is no formal preparation for being a teacher educator in Canada; though, for the last decade the self-study approach has been suggested as a professional development approach for teacher educators (see, for instance, Loughran et al., 2004; Russell & Korthagen, 1995).

of-care-based education—and have illustrated how this end would guide our thinking toward such teacher education. For teacher education to thrive in a changing world, programs need not just adjust to the changes in the local conditions of a changing world—such as greater language and cultural diversity in the Canadian context—but teacher education also needs to actively contribute to the direction in which the world changes. The ethics of care, I suggest here, is appropriate as a response to the view of teaching as a moral enterprise precisely because it provides a direction for living our lives in this world that I would want to promote.

# RESPONSE

## Ruth Kane

Thomas challenges us to consider what teacher education could look like if we take seriously the goal of preparing teachers for "the educating we expect our schools to do" and adopted an ethics-of-care-based approach. This would require us (as teacher educators) to re-frame our work with student teachers so that the emphasis is on student teachers *being* teachers and forming their *identity as teachers* with the goal of supporting their development of the desired agency.

Thomas' proposal would also require us (as teacher educators) to consider what it means to be a teacher educator and to embrace self study as a way of examining and articulating our own ethics-of-care-based agency—this is not something teacher educators have been previously called upon to do and it could meet with significant resistance. However, promise of resistance should never be reason enough not to try. As teacher educators we need to acknowledge that our work is also a moral enterprise—it involves "human action in regard to other human beings" and as such has ethics –of-care-based imperatives at its core. If we, as those concerned with the preparation of teachers, are not able to advocate for teacher education as it could be—grounded in an ethic of care for others and principally for the children and young people who our student teachers will one day teach—then we are falling short of our own potential. I note that Thomas (as do I in my essay) has presented his landscape of teacher education assuming a freedom from the current day institutional and policy structures that tend to constrain program design. While this may seem a little idealistic, it is important to note that Freire reminds us that teachers (and teacher educators) need to use our imagination, creativity, and curiosity if we are to form new social realities and surely this is a key task of educators at all levels.

The notion of beginning with the student teachers' life histories and experiences in an effort to understand the student teachers' needs as learners is important. Such examination needs also to acknowledge the wider contexts within which student teachers' experiences have been formed and to explore the interactions between culture, schooling, the economy, politics, and life experiences that have shaped student teachers' life histories. Through asking critical questions about context, teacher educators could illuminate alternative experiences, and issues of access and equity that many of our student teachers may not have encountered. This may lead to the articulation of a range of ethical and moral positions within teacher education classrooms that would themselves provide useful springboards for considering ways of developing ethics-of-care-based agency.

We invite the reader to consider the following questions:

1. How will our understanding and practice of teacher education change if we ask, "How do we help teacher candidates *become teachers*?" rather than asking, "How do we help teacher candidates *learn to teach*?", thus shifting the focus of our educating from their practice to their being?

2. Both authors promote the argument that teacher education programs need to be grounded in an ethical stance. Their respective elaborations on this argument suggest that teacher educators need to (constantly) "work on themselves" to be able to enact such ethical stances. How do teacher educators *actually* go about this change in their being?

3. In what ways can we re-frame the process of *becoming a teacher* to ensure that we prioritize the values, beliefs, and ethics that guide teachers' decision making and practices regarding children and young people?

4. Using the two preceding essays as a catalyst, develop a set of guiding principles or ethics that could be used for a teacher education program. In collaboration with your colleagues, develop a rationale for each of these principles and explore the implications for teacher education practice.

THEME 3

# The Quality of Field Experience Programs

CONTRIBUTING AUTHORS
Clare Kosnik
Jean-François Desbiens

# It Is Not Just Practice

## Conflicting Goals, Unclear Expectations, Mixed Messages

*Clare Kosnik*

> In the second practicum I had instant rapport with my associate teacher; she made me feel very comfortable. One of the first things she said to me was, "I understand how important this report is, and I don't want you to worry because I'm not going to give you a bad report." She also said, "You know, you're here to learn, you're here to make mistakes; we all make mistakes when we're starting." (Student teacher quoted in Beck & Kosnik, 2002a, p. 81)

The practice teaching component is enshrined in teacher education programs (Glickman & Bey, 1990; McIntyre, Byrd, & Foxx, 1996). For some student teachers it is the place to learn to teach, the "best" part of the program, while for many others it is extremely stressful, an extended endurance test (Britzman, 1991). Many of the problems associated with the practicum are common across programs: locating exemplary practitioners, rewarding associate teachers, providing adequate supervision, and bridging the university program with the practicum (Hagger & McIntyre, 2006). Rather than expound on these challenges, I begin by outlining two sets of problems not typically considered: confusion about the purpose of practice teaching and the complexity of the process. These provide the background to my bold position that we need to reconceptualize the entire practicum component. My arguments are based on many studies I have conducted on aspects of practice teaching (Beck & Kosnik, 2002a; Beck & Kosnik, 2002b; Beck & Kosnik, 2000; Beck et al., 2004; Kosnik & Beck, 2003; Kosnik, 1998), extensive supervision of student teachers, and my long-term work in teacher education.

### Complexity of the Practicum

On the surface, the purpose of the practicum seems quite straightforward—student teachers have the opportunity to learn and improve their skills for instructing and assessing pupils. Yet, the many stakeholders—student teachers, associate (mentor/cooperating/host) teachers, principals, supervisors, and university faculty—are not necessarily in agreement on the goals of the practice teaching. Until we have broader consensus we cannot plan an ideal practicum experience (Kennedy, 2006). The issues described below, many posed as questions, reveal the conflicting goals and cross-purposes of the practicum. I am generalizing and recognize that not all student teachers have these same concerns but they are sufficiently common to be significant.

## Conflicting Goals

Student teachers tend to be anxious about the practicum: Will the pupils like me? Do I have sufficient content knowledge to teach my subjects? Will I get along with my associate teacher? Beyond these basic but substantial issues, there is a hidden set of concerns that are caused by confusion about the goals for the practicum. Are student teachers in the placement to replicate the practices of the associate teacher? Or are they to experiment with new teaching techniques? Are they expected to implement the teaching methods advocated by their professors? As they begin the practicum, they often struggle to find their own teaching style, which some sense may not be consistent with that of their associate teachers. Should they let their own style emerge or try to maintain the associate teacher's practices even if it is uncomfortable to do so? Some quickly realize that schooling has changed since they were students, which leads to soul searching—is teaching the right career choice? Which then mushrooms into another series of questions beginning with: Is this feeling temporary because of the artificiality of the context or is it legitimate?

Should the student teachers reveal their concerns to their associate teacher or supervisor? Can they be trusted? Mature students are placed in a situation where they are the novice. This presents a set of problems including, will my associate teacher be uncomfortable with me because I am older than him/her? Paramount though, for many student teachers, is obtaining a very positive evaluation, which is required if they are to secure a teaching position. They want to improve their teaching practices but they need to get a job because they have mounting debt, want to get married, move out of the house, and so on. How can they navigate the choppy waters of the practicum when it is filled with conflicting messages and unclear goals?

The confusion about roles (and goals) is not limited to student teachers. Some associate teachers unfortunately see the practicum as a time for them to take a break from teaching; while others see their job as ensuring that student teachers experience the harsh reality of teaching (Calderhead & Shorrock, 1997; Maynard, 1996; Williams, 1994). Principals sometimes consider the practicum as an opportunity to identify future staff members, and in other instances want student teachers to teach weak teachers new teaching methods. Some faculty envision the practicum as a place for student teachers to learn the practical aspects of teaching, which relieves them of having to provide tips and strategies in their courses. Practicum supervisors often wonder about their role: Are they to support or evaluate student teachers? (Beck & Kosnik, 2002b; Bullough & Gitlin, 1995; Casey & Howson, 1993). Not surprisingly, the conflicting goals and uncertainty can make the practicum a difficult time for all.

## Layers of Complexity

Learning to teach is not simply a cognitive task, it can engulf students completely. As part of a research study, we surveyed our student teachers asking them to rank the challenges they faced in the practicum. Much to our surprise the majority ranked fatigue as the top challenge. In the semistructured interviews they described the hours and hours they spent preparing lessons. A lesson that might take an experienced teacher thirty minutes to plan took them three hours. When supervising student teachers, I asked them about the time they spent preparing lessons or marking: much to my shock and dismay, many recounted spending five or six hours a night. In some extreme cases, the workload caused physical ailments.

The emotional toll on student teachers can be significant as they struggle to achieve expectations that are often unrealistic or try to interpret mixed messages. In this torrent of emotions, student teachers must quickly build relationships with the pupils and "perform." Trying to please their associate teachers while being scared of failure is stressful. The school culture is often like a black box for them, difficult to figure out, so they retreat into their classrooms, scared to venture into the staff room. They are often dealing with internal conflicts about teaching, including an idealized vision of themselves as teachers that is shattered in the harsh reality of teaching.

The learning curve during the practicum is staggering: acquiring procedural knowledge (e.g., names of students, administrative procedures) *while* learning to teach. Associate teachers have many responsibilities because their work with student teachers is simply added to their other duties; this often forces them to give feedback in spurts and starts, which can confuse student teachers or not provide the guidance they need to develop.

## Reconceptualizing the Practicum

The dysfunctional nature of many practice teaching placements will not be rectified by simply tinkering with some of the procedures. We need to entirely reconceptualize practice teaching, beginning with a new overarching goal that is both compelling and all-encompassing. This should be something like: the goal of practice teaching is to support pupil learning. Some might argue that pupil learning is inherent in practice teaching, but it needs to be at the forefront of all discussions. This shift in focus from the student teacher to the pupils would alter many of the problematic dynamics within placements, in part recasting the work of the associate teacher as a mentor (not simply a "host" teacher) with the student teachers as apprentices. In apprenticeships the goal is to produce the best product, which is achieved by the mentor and mentee working closely together towards a common goal. The learning occurs as the mentee works alongside the mentor and under close supervision. If the product is not of the highest quality, the customer will be dissatisfied. In our case, the "product" would be maximized pupil learning. Practice teaching would become a time for associate and student teachers to jointly develop powerful learning experiences for pupils. I will now outline some of the implications of my position and further describe it.

Increased Funding

Universities do not typically invest heavily in the practice teaching component of the program but this must change. Increased funds alone will not solve the problem of the practicum nor will paying associate teachers a substantial amount of money (although it would help to recognize their work and time). Funds need to be spent on training associate teachers to be strong mentors. Workshop topics should include working collaboratively, easing the transition into teaching, and teaching about teaching; and these discussions should be accompanied with sessions on pedagogical strategies that support pupil learning. Having a dual focus—mentoring and teaching practices—would support teachers' professional development, thus ensuring student teachers are placed with exemplary practitioners.

Increased funding is needed so that associate teachers can be relieved of their teaching duties to spend time co-planning with student teachers on a regular basis, as described below. Time must be built into each day for feedback. Being an associate teacher must not be in addition to all other duties, they must be relieved of some of their responsibilities.

The Place of the Practicum in the Program

There are many different models for the practicum: extended blocks of time during the academic year (e.g., six-week placements); frequent short placements (e.g., three weeks); a long placement at the end of the academic program (e.g., three months). Yet each has a central flaw: the practicum is conceptualized as a self-contained experience. In keeping with the apprenticeship concept and the focus on pupil learning, student teachers need to be in their placements for the entire school year. Whether the model is two or three days a week or half a day every day, the experience must span the entire year, so student teachers can witness the pupils' progress and be fully involved in the ten-month school year. This would naturally link theory and practice, allow student teachers time to have graduated responsibility, and relieve the pressure on associate teachers to evaluate student teachers in a short period of time.

My proposed model would create challenges for schools of education in smaller communities where there may be insufficient placements in neighbouring schools. This may require satellite campuses, which would have funding implications for the school of education. Further, the practicum should not be organized for the convenience of student teachers, such as teaching in a school in their hometown in order to live at home during the practicum (even if it is a significant distance from the university). Rather it should be conceptualized as part of the day-to-day teacher education program, thus making the program seamless. This model allows student teachers ongoing opportunities to talk about their learning about teaching. Debriefing that is held at the end of the practicum has limited value because student teachers cannot return to their placement to try out new classroom management techniques. Debriefing in this proposed model would occur weekly, allowing student teachers to immediately rectify teaching problems or refocus their energies.

School and University *IN* Partnership

With the shift in focus to pupil learning, the relationship between the school and the university becomes of paramount importance. The professional development school model is one that resonates strongly with my views for a reconceptualized practicum. Rather than reiterate the elements, strengths, and weaknesses of this model, I want to consider a few other aspects. In Toronto, it is common for more than one faculty of education to place student teachers in the same school, which is problematic (e.g., different evaluation procedures) and makes building a partnership difficult (e.g., splitting staff among different universities). As I envision it, the school would recognize one particular faculty of education as its partner in the enterprise of educating pupils. There would need to be a commitment from both institutions to the partnership, with regular communication and shared goals.

This model has significant implications for funding (e.g., financial support for partnership), workload for faculty, and rewards for faculty (e.g., recognition of partnership work during tenure review). Schools would become the "clinics" for the academic program. Just as teaching hospitals have rounds led by senior doctors, schools would be the sites for faculty to conduct rounds where they deconstruct exemplary teaching practices or show theory in practice. The faculty's work would not be restricted to the university but would span two settings, which could exacerbate the already significant problem of workload for those in preservice. In these professional development–type schools, both teachers and student teachers would have the possibility of being involved in research, either led by a faculty member or initiated on their own (e.g., action research). Involvement in research and/or sharing research findings would help teachers improve their practice, which in turn would enhance pupil learning. The research questions faculty investigate could include those that are critically important to teachers.

## A Mentorship Relationship

With student teachers placed in school for the entire year, the relationship between the individual student teacher and associate teacher would have time to blossom into a solid partnership. Additionally, student teachers would have many opportunities to observe and work with other teachers in the department or division. The urgency for student teachers to learn "everything" so that they can quickly teach independently would be removed. Central to the relationship between the associate teacher and student teacher would be co-planning. As we have discovered in our research (Kosnik & Beck, 2007), program planning is one of the most challenging aspects for new teachers. During the practicum, they need to have a "window" into their associate teachers' thinking about program planning: how they do it, how they decide what to teach, and how they prioritize.

Much of the practicum in its current form has the student teacher planning lessons independently and oftentimes not having access to the associate teacher's resources, which leaves a novice developing lessons that may be of questionable value, often soldiering on in isolation. After jointly planning, the student teacher may teach the whole class or the associate teacher may be the sole instructor, but much of the time the class is split into two groups, with each teacher working with one group of pupils.

With student teachers in the placement for the entire year, the associate and student teachers could experiment with new teaching strategies or use time-tested ones. The pressure on student teachers to be innovative or independent would be lessened; however, innovation would occur naturally. And in the university program, focus on instruction on program planning would draw on the expertise of the classroom teachers and not simply be taught as an abstract concept. I have long felt we need to rethink the ways we teach student teachers to plan; in our current system the tyranny of the formal lesson plan reigns. Student teachers often complete lengthy templates that do not help them learn a method for planning that can be sustained during the busy first years of teaching. Working closely with practicing teachers would allow them to identify a realistic model for lesson and unit planning.

## Concluding Comments

The framework that I have described above is ambitious and would require a significant level of commitment from all stakeholders. I do not underestimate the work and challenge of completely reconceptualizing the practicum. The current format may work in some cases but overall it does not sufficiently prepare beginning teachers. In a research study, *Teacher Education for Literacy Teaching*, we followed graduates from teacher education through their first three years of teaching. For some, this initial period was horrendous, with survival being their immediate goal. This is ideal neither for their well-being nor for their pupils. Teacher education often sits at the margins of schooling. We need to move it squarely into the school arena while still capitalizing on the talents and interests of faculty. The research activities and the extensive subject knowledge of faculty when shared with teachers could enhance all aspects of schooling, leading to increased pupil learning. My proposal is not for the faint of heart, nor does it solve all the problems listed in the first section of this essay. To implement it would require courage, tenacity, flexibility, openness, funding, leadership, compromise, and a sense of humour. It may take years to reconceptualize the practicum component of teacher education, but the education of our children should be our foremost concern. Preparing all teachers to have the skills, knowledge, and attitudes to work with a diverse student population is a daunting task. It requires the teacher education enterprise to be guided by a vision for learning. My vision focuses on the learning of the student teachers, pupils, associate teachers, and faculty.

# RESPONSE

## *Jean-François Desbiens*

Discussions about practice teaching can be related, to some extent, to the teaching activity itself: it quickly becomes obvious that this can be done only while referring to specific practice contexts. Nevertheless, Clare Kosnik was successful in underlining several problems that seem to show, in a persistent and rather transcendent way, the various contexts in which teachers' practical training is updated. For example, Clare seems to get it right when she bemoans the lack of a clear consensus regarding practice-teaching goals. Clare also notes that the same situation prevails in the coexistence of several practice-teaching designs that may appear contradictory, if not incompatible, a situation which leads to significant challenges for the professional development of student teachers. Finally, I have no choice but to agree with Clare when she asserts that it is necessary to better define the function of cooperative teachers and put more energy and resources into the training of these professionals. Aren't they responsible both for training qualified teachers and for ensuring the progression of students' skills and knowledge acquisition?

Clare supports the thesis that promotes a reexamination of practical training basics. She consistently suggests numerous solutions likely to improve these basics. I particularly endorse her idea of putting pupil and teacher-trainee learning back into the centre of the supervision process. This is, to my point of view, her most appealing argument. Its apparent simplicity, however, shouldn't deceive us. Let us recall that the professional development of teachers goes through some long stages and that signs of regression can sometimes be seen. Initially self-centered and concentrated on defining and assuming their new identity, trainees must gradually become more aware of their pupils' needs. Only then is it necessary for student teachers to learn how to decode their own needs. Anyone who attends closely to the trainees' progression will note their oscillations between establishing group control through the assertion of their status and their motivation from constraint, and their expression of interest in and providing assistance to their pupils' learning process. It is hoped that, from one training course to another, these oscillations will become more finely attuned to the requirements posed by varying situations. This would not only indicate an evolution in the trainees' concerns but also in their capacity to modulate their interventions. For many trainees, however, pupils' learning targets can prove to be a challenge that may go beyond their proximal development zone.

It takes years to develop a good teacher but only a few seconds to destroy one. The identification of realistic developmental targets is essential, as is the proposal for meaningful experiments allowing their implementation. "Learning all the ropes" is part of what is learned in teacher education programs, along with the development of effective teaching professionals. Thus, any effort at reconceptualization should not be limited to practical training. This issue is clearly significant, and I still think it is essential to inject more resources into cooperative teachers' training.

# Practical Training Must Be More than Just Good Will in the Field

*Jean-François Desbiens*

## Introduction

In a report published in the early 2000s, the Organization for Economic Co-operation and Development (OECD) stated that teacher quality is a strong priority since their function is inseparable from the success of the educational enterprise and the requirements imposed on teachers are ever increasing. More recently, OECD emphasized that the quality of teachers is the primary variable affecting student achievement that is under the control of educational decision-makers. There are significant differences in quality among teachers that give rise to discriminatory, and above all, cumulative effects on students' academic success.

Major teaching reforms recently initiated in Europe, North America, Latin America, and Oceania (Borges & Desbiens, 2003) suggest that professionalizing teaching requires raising both the intellectual standards and the quality of professional training as well as identifying a core knowledge base to establish a scientific foundation for the profession (Gauthier et al., 1997). These reforms have furthered the adoption of competency-based approaches in initial teacher preparation and have increased supervised student teaching to nearly 700 hours in Québec, Canada. By so doing, these reforms have revealed some difficulties and limitations faced by student teachers during their practice teaching as well as exposed many of the tensions surrounding the roles and tasks of cooperating teachers. I will focus on these dual aspects throughout the text.

## Training Teachers through Practice: Putting Together Efficiency Requirements

Practical training, commonly described as the defining period in teacher training, requires critical reflection. Regarded as the culmination of the teacher training process (Jordan, Phillips & Brown, 2004), the teaching practice is an experience that can deeply affect an individual (Tardif & Lessard, 1999). Several studies have shown that new and experienced teachers think their initial teaching practice is a key aspect of their professional preparation, mainly because this experience allows them to become familiar with the complex dynamics of schools and teaching. It also allows them to learn more about efficient teaching strategies as well as their ability to implement them (OECD, 2005).

Several researchers and cooperating teachers have suggested that it is desirable to introduce the practical training very early in the initial training so that it will be closely and coherently coupled with the theoretical. This is needed to help future teachers develop appropriate teaching behaviours (Brawdy & Byra, 1995), foster their reflexive skills through systematic training (Talvitie, Peltokallio & Männistö, 2000), and gain practical knowledge, without which the matching of professional actions with real-life situations may be compromised.

However, other researchers are now reviewing the usefulness of internships during initial training. Calderhead, for example, has demonstrated that teacher trainees resist change because of their convictions and because they perceive their own judgments as superficial and pragmatic (Calderhead, 1987). Teacher trainees would then quickly reach a plateau in their professional learning process and would tend to imitate traditional practices. Chaliès & Durand (2000) report that practical training experiences are often inconsistent because their objectives are unclear and poorly harmonized with theory or because these experiences underline deficiencies in work-planning and in the specification of roles and responsibilities for teacher trainees and cooperating teachers.

Any inadequacy in or even lack of professional qualifications, competencies, and beliefs in a cooperating teacher will likely limit the impact of practical training. For example, such training can cause extremely strong dissonance in the student teachers' minds if they perceive too great a contradiction between what their program conveys and what their cooperating teachers advocate in the school environment. Student teachers can also be inhibited by feelings of discomfort and incompetence if they have to confront many difficult situations that they are not yet equipped to address. Cooperating teachers who demonstrate lower levels of competency with respect to pedagogical supervision do not provide the student teacher with as productive a learning experience as they deserve and can even hinder their professional development (Rikard & Veal, 1996).

## Acknowledging the Cooperating Teacher Position: What It Already Offers and What It Has in Store

According to Copas, "The job of the cooperating teacher is to help the student teacher develop a deep and meaningful concept of teaching, to help the student teacher analyze the many facets of teaching, to provide the student teacher with sources and resources, and to encourage the student teacher's unique teaching behaviour" (1984, in Koster, Korthagen, & Wubbels, 1998, p. 76). Numerous studies agree that cooperating teachers strongly influence the professional development of future teachers (McIntyre & Byrd, 1998; Mitchell & Schwager, 1993; Talvitie, Peltokallio & Männistö, 2000). These student teachers are actively shaping their beliefs (Hastings, 2004), and their practice substantially affects their orientations, aptitudes, conceptions, and teaching practices (Talvitie et al., 2000). Cooperating teachers' comments and advice are perceived as being more useful and straightforward than those provided by university trainers (Koster et al., 1998). Cooperating teachers are often viewed as the ones who inspire student teachers to become teachers. Considering what has previously been mentioned, it is surprising that education stakeholders, in general, have given so little consideration to defining cooperating teachers' institutional and socioprofessional status, their actual incorporation into teacher-trainer teams, their formal education and training, and the evaluation of their skills, as well as their selection for a key position regarding initial training (Chaliès & Durand, 2000; Koster et al., 1998; OECD, 2005; Rikard & Veal, 1996).

## Training of Cooperating Teachers: A Requirement for Competency

The learning of the teaching profession is full of persistent myths (Brunelle & Brunelle, 1999). Without questioning and bringing out the required nuances, the perpetuation of these myths can discredit the contributions of professional training and research in teacher education. Furthermore, unsuitable conceptions of the role of the field experience can also be conveyed. These myths are embodied in the following beliefs: the ability to teach is innate rather than acquired; teaching skills are technical in nature and the field experience is thus a time to put into practice learned skills and knowledge; teaching skills are of a mechanical nature and problems encountered by teacher trainees are solved by imitating the cooperating teacher's solutions; and teaching skills are best acquired through experience, therefore, regardless of the supervision they received, teacher trainees will develop their own practical skills. It seems to me, these debatable beliefs should be the subject of open discussions during cooperating teachers' training sessions before they are confirmed as mentors—because they will inevitably influence the learning conditions offered to student teachers.

However, such initiatives are rare and little supported. And, judging their appropriateness is difficult. A recent study conducted in Québec by Lacroix-Roy, Lessard, and Garant (2003) found, notably, that 81.5% of cooperating teachers received less than thirty hours of training, with the average being 14.8 hours. This puzzles me, considering the emphasis given to initial teacher training. This perplexity is deepened by the ostensible ambivalence of the COFPE (*Comité d'orientation de la formation du personnel enseignant du Québec*)[1] (2005, p. 39). The COFPE has stated that it may be necessary to promote "compliance with competence standards" rather than "compliance with training standards." Unless we subscribe to empiricism regarding teacher training, how is it possible to separate competence standards and training standards? If we acknowledge the importance of training, what should the contents and conditions be, knowing that, as in the outcomes of teaching preparation, a washout effect might also be observed in the practice of supervision (Boudreau & Baria, 1998)?

## Defining Specific Competencies for a Unique Teaching Function

Supervising student teachers may require a specific expertise that is quite different from that required to teach (Gervais, 1997). Becoming a cooperating teacher basically means to embrace parallel approaches to identity that are quite different from those used by a regular teacher (COFPE, 2005). Cooperating teachers must have a technical expertise, thorough knowledge of human behaviour, and leadership, as well as good conceptual and organizational skills (Bujold, 2002). Cooperating teachers must also be able to read and analyse the level of professional development of teaching candidates in order to identify their needs and fulfill them, notably by implementing proper learning conditions (Wiles and Bondi, 2000). Their capacity to involve the teacher trainees in a reflexive analysis of their professional activities seems also to be pivotal according to several authors (Brunelle, Drouin, Godbout & Tousignant, 1988; Brunelle & Brunelle, 1999; Carlier, 2002; Desbiens, Brunelle, Spallanzani & Roy, 2006, Desbiens, Spallanzani, Brunelle, Turcotte & Roy, 2006; Ministère de l'Éducation, 1994; Normand-Guérette, 1998). Also pivotal are their abilities to evaluate teacher trainees (Brunelle, Drouin, Godbout & Tousignant, 1988; Brunelle & Brunelle, 1999; Desbiens, Brunelle, Spallanzani & Roy, 2006; Ministère de l'Éducation, 1994; Normand-Guérette, 1998) and to motivate and give them confidence (Carlier, 2002; Desbiens, Brunelle, Spallanzani & Roy, 2006). All these capacities seem relevant to me. Others could be added. However, a question is raised here: How should we gather together these sparse elements to create a super-

---

[1] Committee on Teacher Training in Québec; our translation.

vision training program that is coherent and meaningful and specifically intended for cooperating teachers?

## Defining Our Future: It Is Up to Us to Achieve It Now!

If today the quality of teachers is a priority, as claimed by the OECD (2001), why is so little energy devoted to the training and supervision of cooperating teachers—the individuals largely responsible for this initial teacher training? This goal should be shared not only by cooperating teachers but also by all concerned with the teaching profession. Therefore, shouldn't there be an urgent and serious consultation on the search for shared solutions?

Generally speaking, I believe the elements presented here point toward too great a tolerance on the part of government authorities, schooling institutions, and teachers' associations for the inconsistency, amateurism, and improvisation of the teacher training program. Do we always need to wait for a crisis before trying to improve things?

First and foremost, total commitment from the teacher trainee, whose human and learning experiences form the central part of the commitment, is the key to the success of the training course. However, in my opinion, the cooperating teachers also play a key role in the decisions to be made regarding the work-related learning conditions they will provide for student teachers. Some of these decisions include the approach they take to the supervisory process; their classroom practices and interactions with pupils; the quality, frequency, and nature of the regulation episodes they provide for student teachers; the intensity of the reflexive process that will eventually lead to student teachers' professional autonomy; and the attention they pay to the evolution of the student teachers' perceptions towards the profession.

Isn't investing in the training and supervision of cooperating teachers a smart way to renew the teaching methods for practical training? Isn't this also a great opportunity to establish a healthy and productive "vertical collegiality structure"[2] among all the trainers, which would benefit all student teachers and tomorrow's entire teaching profession?

I believe it is essential that the role of cooperating teachers become more professionalized. To achieve this, we must afford it institutional and socioprofessional recognition, clearly define its scope of intervention, describe a competency system of reference, and last but not least, provide appropriate training.

---

[2] Vertical collegiality structure: Professors in universities, CEGEPs and teachers at the elementary and secondary levels are united in a common purpose and respect each other's abilities to work toward that purpose.

# RESPONSE

## *Clare Kosnik*

Jean-François Desbiens' extremely interesting essay, *Practical Training Must Be More than Just Good Will in the Field*, scratches beneath the surface of the practicum to expose some of the pitfalls that often await vulnerable and naïve student teachers. He rightly argues that practice teaching is an extremely important aspect of learning to become a teacher; yet for some, this experience is not necessarily educative and may even be detrimental to their well-being. How should we proceed? Jean-François suggests that we need to improve the practices of the cooperating teacher if we are to significantly improve the teacher education program.

The complexity of the role of the cooperating teacher is often unacknowledged. In our hurry to secure a sufficient number of field experience placements, we may not consider the teacher's ability to mentor a student teacher. Jean-François suggests that "cooperating teachers must have a technical expertise, thorough knowledge of human behaviour, and leadership as well as good conceptual and organizational skills." He adds that cooperating teachers "must also be able to read and analyze the level of professional development of the candidates in order to identify their needs." He rightly argues that being a cooperating teacher requires a different skill set than that for teaching children. Helping a student teacher learn involves much more than simply sharing resources or providing an opportunity to teach a group of children.

Jean-François reveals the inconsistencies in the rhetoric about the practicum. It is regarded as an extremely critical component of the teacher education program yet we continue to place students with underprepared associate teachers. The contradictions are glaring yet they persist. Why? Is it simply a matter of finances? I think that finances are only part of the problem. We do not have a sufficiently credible body of research to show the difference that effective associate teachers can make in student teachers' learning. Without solid research, we cannot even begin to debunk the myths that swirl around teacher education (e.g., an associate teacher simply needs to be a "good" teacher). Secondly, many of those who supervise the practicum are part-time contract instructors or graduate students; neither have a voice at the decision-making table and they may not understand the complexity of their role and that of the associate teacher.

# We invite the reader to consider the following questions:

1. Is the university's unwillingness to address issues around the role of the cooperating teacher symptomatic of our lack of clear goals for teacher education programs?

2. Should cooperating teachers encourage replication of their own practice or nurture the individual talents of student teachers? How would either of these goals be attained?

3. What would an effective training program for cooperating teachers and supervisors encompass and over what period of time?

4. Is it better to limit supervision training to technical interventions, such as observation, feedback, and reinforcement, or to tie training more closely to conceptual models that are likely to provide food for thought and action?

THEME 4

# Responding to Diversity and Demands for Social Justice

CONTRIBUTING AUTHORS

Claudia Mitchell

Vianne Timmons

# "This has nothing to do with us—or does it?"

## Youth as Knowledge Producers in Addressing HIV and AIDS in a Canadian Preservice Education Program

*Claudia Mitchell*

> HIV/AIDS presents the greatest learning challenge to education systems. In the past, the consequences of failure to learn involved simply a delay in progress from one academic level to another or confinement (sometimes temporary) to a lower socio-economic order. With HIV/AIDS the consequence of pedagogic failure is terminal. (Charles, 1999)

### The Context

"It shames and diminishes us all," writes Stephen Lewis in his role as UN Envoy on HIV and AIDS. He is commenting on the desperate situation globally as a result of the AIDS pandemic, and the unwillingness of many governments and citizens of the West to take this seriously. Lewis' passionate words in his many talks across Canada and around the world and in his recent book, *Race against Time*, implore people to care as global citizens and to overcome what might be read as "this has nothing to do with us."

HIV/AIDS is now recognized as a global crisis, particularly among youth, with young women emerging as the most vulnerable group (Commonwealth Secretariat, 2002; Gomez & Meacham, 1998; UNAIDS, 2006). As Stephen Lewis, the UN Envoy on HIV/AIDS stated at the recent International AIDS conference in Bangkok, "It's a pandemic within a pandemic"—with girls and young women making up 75 percent of those between the ages of 15 and 24 who are infected (2004). In KwaZulu-Natal, a province in South Africa that is at the epicentre of the disease, current estimates say between 37 and 47 percent of all women are HIV positive. China, Russia, and parts of the Caribbean, particularly Jamaica, are other countries that are experiencing new levels of urgency. The epidemic in the Caribbean is second in magnitude only to Sub-Saharan Africa.

Compared to countries in sub-Saharan Africa, sexual health and HIV rates in Canada seem low. In 2007, an estimated 58,000 Canadians were reported to be living with HIV or AIDS (Public Health Agency of Canada, 2007). This is compared to an estimated 22 million HIV positive people in the Sub-Saharan region (AVERT, 2008). However, new infections in Canada have risen 15% from 2002 and this is mainly within the heterosexual/non-endemic exposure category (Public Health Agency of Canada, 2007). This means that , HIV is no longer the "gay disease" nor is it relegated only to "high risk" communities like intravenous drug users or transsexual sex workers. As in other parts of the world, HIV has an ever-increasing effect on women and young girls. In Canada girls between the ages of 15 and 29 represent one of the largest growing populations within the epidemic (Public Health Agency of Canada, 2006). As a whole, aboriginal people are over represented within the HIV epidemic and almost a third of the new infections between 1998 and 2006 are among aboriginal people below 30 years old (Public Health Agency of Canada, 2007). Chlamydia rates amongst youth are rising and rates of gonorrhoea are highest amongst youth under the age of 25 (McKay, 2004). In general, youth are unaware of the prevalence of sexually transmitted infections (STIs) and have many misconceptions with regards to their possible long-term consequences (Frappier & Canadian Association for Adolescent Health, 2006; Public Health Agency of Canada, 2006). For example, a large proportion of Canadian youth falsely believe there is a cure or vaccine for HIV and AIDS (Public Health Agency of Canada, 2006).

The issue of "this has nothing to do with us" is at the heart of this essay about my work with new teachers in Canada, specifically Québec, where the HIV/AIDS statistics are particularly alarming. Seventy-four percent of Québec youth between the ages of 15 and 24 report having sexual intercourse. Yet a startling 52 percent of young women there did not use a condom the last time they had sex (Rotermann, 2005). The Canada Youth Sexual Health & HIV/AIDS study (CYSHHAS) reports that "2/3 of Quebec students in grade seven, half of students in grade nine, and one third of students in grade eleven do not know that there is no cure for HIV & AIDS." In 2000, Québec was one of four provinces to have a teen pregnancy rate above the national average.

I am interested in how work on sexuality and HIV and AIDS—an issue of health and behavior but also one of poverty, race, gender, geography, and so on—can help us address social justice in teacher education. As someone who works in narrative and young adult literature, I am particularly interested in how young adult literature can introduce the question "this has nothing to do with us—or does it?"

## The Project: Preservice Teacher, HIV and AIDS, and Taking Action

As part of a young adult literature elective for preservice teachers, my class works with three novels that address HIV and AIDS: Deborah Ellis' *The Heaven Shop*, Alan Stratton's *Chanda's Secret,* and Bernice Adams' *Nancy's Secret*. The first two are written by Canadian authors and address HIV and AIDS in sub-Saharan Africa. Both are based on extensive fieldwork each author conducted in the region. *Nancy's Secret*, written by an American author, tells the story of a young white woman in the U.S. who becomes infected as a result of unprotected sex. The students read the novels and we engage in a number of close reading activities. I have also had Deborah Ellis visit the class so she can discuss her fieldwork *The Heaven Shop* with Canadian youths. In addition, an interview with Ellis is embedded in her novel, which helps create a sense that Canadians can do something.

Along the way the students also view two video documentaries: *Fire and Hope* (Walsh & Mitchell, 2004), a documentary about young people who are AIDS activists in Khaleletisha and Atlantis, two townships outside Cape Town providing an urban hip-hop graffiti picture of South African youth; and *Our Photos, Our Videos, Our Stories* (Mak, Mitchell & Stuart, 2005), a documentary on the use of photos, voice, and video to address HIV and AIDS in a deeply rural part of South Africa.

The novels, complemented by the two documentaries, are our entry point—the core material—the rest is up to the students. The deep-reading group-project assignment, as I call it, is quite simple:

> Now that you have read the 3 novels, embark upon a deep-reading project. It could be a curriculum project or an action-oriented project. You can write your own set of short stories on a related issue, conduct informal interviews, create a game ... [ellipsis intentional] Each group will have 10 minutes to present their work to the class and can hand in what seems the most appropriate representation of the project.

It is possibly the most unstructured assignment I have ever given in 25 years of working with new teachers—and possibly the most successful.

Over three years of using renditions of this assignment with nearly 300 students, I have seen a vast range of responses, and almost all of them have gone far beyond what I would have received from a tighter assignment. These have included the adaptation of the TV show *Who Wants to Be a Mil-*

*lionaire*, the adaptation of the famous board game Trivial Pursuit as Sexual Pursuit (Figure 1), and even digital games for young people (teachers or adolescents) to assess their own knowledge of HIV and AIDS. Many of the students who devised these projects admitted they hadn't realized how little they actually knew themselves. What they say is "it really opened up our eyes."

Some, inspired by the role of fiction and the power of the novels, experiment with writing their own young adult fiction (short stories and novellas) or poetry on local themes of their choosing, such as the high incidence of HIV and AIDS amongst aboriginal youth. Others create a magazine to show how youth friendly, relevant material on these issues can be addressed. (Figure 2) Still others work with various Web tools: creating a Facebook link, Web sites (about novels, about facts and organizations for Québec young people, etc.), and so on.

Figure 1

Figure 2

Still others implement projects that directly involve youth. One group, for example, that is already involved in an after-school program, screens *Fire and Hope* and invites local adolescents to respond and in a sense "storyboard" their own documentary on what needs to be looked at by Canadian youth. Another group decides to conduct an awareness campaign by cycling from one end of Montreal Island to the other, carrying "HIV and AIDS Awareness in Québec" placards. They are particularly inspired by the bicycle references in *Chanda's Secrets* and *The Heaven Shop* The bicycle, they discover, is not just transportation but also a symbol of going beyond the village. And it represents new possibilities for spreading the word in training. Along the way they interview young people. One of their group films the whole project, and the group turns the footage into a short documentary that is presented in class. Based on their findings (that a lot of young people don't know much about AIDS, despite its presence in their own communities), they create their own blog. Another group, all students enrolled in physical education, organize a fun-run in a small town. They each wear their own home-produced T-shirts with appropriate messages on HIV and AIDS.

Taken together, these projects (and their presentation to the whole class) demonstrate to the student teachers themselves a range of issues. Most acknowledge they had no idea how little they knew about STIs and HIV and AIDS. This, I would argue, effectively shows the power of "starting with ourselves." Many confirm what my teacher educator colleagues in South Africa have found: "young people are often sick of hearing about AIDS," and it is a challenge to engage people to work with the issues. I have been struck by how many students actually become involved in organizations on campus or in the community—and, critically, how many do follow-up activities in their student teaching.

## Youth as Knowledge Producers: Framing Participatory Work with Preservice Teachers

The argument has been made elsewhere that, given so many new teachers are themselves youths (under the age of 24) or youth-based in their orientation (planning to work with adolescents) there is a compelling rationale to draw on the emerging work on youth as knowledge producers in framing curriculum within teacher education (Mitchell, Weber & Yoshida, 2008; Stuart & Mitchell, 2007). The term "youth as knowledge producers" describes the body of work that involves youth as producers of new arts media (e.g., drumming, hip-hop graffiti, photography, video documentary, radio, writing, and so on) in the context of HIV and AIDS education. The use of the term draws on the work of Lankshear and Knobel (2003).

While the work is derived from the broader study of arts-based research (Cole, Knowles & Luciano, 2004; Knowles and Cole, 2007) and relates to the use of art in health education, work with youth and HIV and AIDS has become its own research area, as a recent study for UNESCO of several hundred organizations around the world attests (Mitchell, Low & Hoechsmann, 2006; Gould and Marsh, 2004). Organizations such as UNICEF and UNESCO have warned that unless youth are given a more significant role in producing locally relevant messages, prevention programs are doomed to failure (Ford, Oddalo & Chorlton, 2003). Such a position recognizes that although young people are sometimes victims of an invincible attitude that says "it can never happen to me," simultaneously they are more likely to believe they can make change. And while there may be AIDS fatigue (Mitchell & Smith, 2003), youths are more likely to want to do something! As Pattman demonstrates (2006) in studying with young people their sexual identities, the idea of youth as knowledge producers also positions youth as assets to each other.

To date much of this work has been tested in South Africa, involving preservice teachers, as an often understudied, "youth-based" population (Stuart & Mitchell, 2007), along with working with young people in schools and communities. In studies focusing on youth and HIV, we have tested photo-voice (Mitchell et al., 2005; Moletsane et al., 2007), participatory video (Mitchell, C., De Lange, N, Moletsane, R., Stuart, J., Taylor, M. and Buthelezi, T., in press; Mak, 2006), collage (Norris et al., 2007), drawing (Stuart, 2006; Mitchell, Walsh & Moletsane, 2006), and hip-hop and forum theatre (Stuart & Mitchell, 2007).

In one project, beginning teachers participated in a series of arts-based HIV and AIDS workshops as part of a Guidance and Counselling module (Stuart, 2004; 2007). In another, a group of beginning teachers as peer educators on the campus of the University of KwaZulu-Natal have been involved in a series of 'youth as knowledge producers' workshops on video, photo-voice, forum theater, and hip-hop to address HIV and AIDS. These beginning teachers have been working in rural schools with grade 9 and 10 learners (Stuart & Mitchell, 2007). The studies span both rural and urban settings and offer the possibility for examining both short-term impact as well as impact over several years beyond the life of a project. These include the *Soft Cover* project (Walsh & Mitchell, 2006; Mitchell, 2006), as well as a series of interventions in Swaziland and in the Vulindlela district of KwaZulu-Natal. These projects can also be viewed in the context of a Media Education orientation where there is growing recognition of the value of positioning learners as producers (Buckingham, 2003; Buckingham & Sefton-Green, 1994).

Early on in the emergence of media education much of the focus was on arming youth against what was seen as the corruptive influence of media and "common " culture, but as the discipline matured this focus was balanced by a recognition that critical awareness, and (arguably) empowerment, could result when media production was encouraged. By producing their own media texts, whether through the traditional print media like newspapers, visual media such as photographs, audio media such as radio, or, in line with global communication development, new media—Web sites, chat rooms, and blogging—young people could give voice to their own ideas and interact with people in ever-widening social and cultural circles.

What connects these various project areas are the following:

(1) Commitment to the use of creative/artistic tools of expression. These tools include the spoken word, graffiti, hip-hop, radio drama, photography, video, rave culture, comics, literature, zines, kwaito, dancing, forum theater, and storytelling.
(2) Personal (and often group) reflection and engagement through participation (although participation itself can be defined in a number of ways and vary in terms of level).
(3) Meaning and relevance to participants.
(4) Some mechanism for taking action in terms of personal and group empowerment as well as individual and social action.

Drawing on the work of Griffiths et al. (2003), Cochran-Smith (2004), and others, what this work suggests is a more nuanced view of what social justice can look like (literally) in a teacher education program.

## Critical Spaces? Action Spaces?

But I do not want to minimize the challenges of youth-as-knowledge-producer initiatives nor the significance of seizing on the critical spaces that this kind of work opens up. To return to the deep-reading assignment, there is a range of issues that emerge that can be taken up through class discussion, reflection in journals, out-of-class discussion, and so on. How, for example, does one address what might appear to be the "do-gooder" mentality, which can ignore the structural features of poverty, gender, and geography associated with HIV and AIDS? Some wonder why authors like Ellis and Stratton are writing about Africa. Why aren't they documenting stories in Canada? Others question the appropriateness of outsiders writing about Africa. Arguably, awareness is a beginning but it can't be the end, so it is critical that there are strategies in place for people to move forward. Many teachers worry that even though they have seen the relevance of this work to Canadian young people, they worry they will not be allowed to bring up such issues in their own student teaching, and that schools (or the parents or the students themselves) will be resistant or see no relevance. One way of addressing these concerns is to make sure the project doesn't end with the presentations and that there is a "finale" after the presentations where teachers debate questions such as "What difference could this type of work make in schools?," "What are some strategic areas for entry in schools?," "How does one get buy-in from the schools?," and "How does anyone make a difference?"

As I describe below, this last question took centre-stage on the last evening of the course the third time I conducted this project:

*The last night of the class. Where has the term gone? We form a massive circle to accommodate the 85 students. Each has a minute or two to say something about their learning in the course. I tell them they talk about whatever they want: do a dramatic reading, say something that they have been dying to say all term and never had a chance, talk briefly about their final individual project for the course.*

*The 4 aboriginal women in the class ask if they can do something as a group and at the very end. They are a little older than most of the students in the class—indeed some of them are mothers of teenagers—and they have already captured the hearts and minds of the rest of the class through a presentation earlier in the term which used drumming and chanting. Their turn comes. It is late and I am aware that everyone is now getting anxious to get going. But everyone stays.*

*We see the drums again and the blanket they had introduced in their presentation earlier in the term. Nellie speaks: "All term we have talked about making a difference and being aware of the needs of others. In our community we have a tradition. When someone is in financial need, we come together. We chant and drum and as we do we pass the blanket. Everyone puts in what they can and then we present the proceeds to the person who needs it. It might be money but it could be something else. Throughout the term we have talked so much about Africa and we know Dr. Mitchell has projects there. We know that they need money but we also know that they need lots of things—even pencils or notebooks. We are going to pass the blanket. Just put in what you can."*

*And then they begin. Nellie and Jean carry the blanket around the circle. Beth chants and Yvonne drums. The room is filled with sound. The whole procedure probably only takes 3 minutes but it as though time has stopped. Finally they come around to me and present the blanket full of loonies, toonies, bills . . . It is so moving. (My fieldnotes, November 28, 2008)*

But it doesn't end there. When I come to look at their final assignments I notice that people have added in packages of new pens, duotang covers, and notebooks—slipped in to their folders. Sometimes there is a note but most times the materials are just there. And then I read something in one of the reflective logs that totally captivates me. The student is reflecting on that final class as well. She writes: "What these women showed us is that we can (and must) go beyond awareness. It can be very small but we can always do something. We just have to be imaginative. And I now know that's what I want to do and what I want my students to see."

## Acknowledgments

I would like to thank the students enrolled in Young Adult Literature at McGill University in the Fall Semester 2005, Fall Semester 2006, and Fall

Semester 2007, for their enthusiastic and thoughtful participation. In particular I would like to thank the 'Ssexual Puruits' group and the 'Explain' group for the use of their images in this article. I also wish to thank the National Research Foundation for the Youth as Knowledge Producers project 2007–2009 (with Jean Stuart, PI; Naydene De Lange, Relebohile Moletsane, Rob Pattmann, Thabisile Buthelezi) for their generous funding.

# RESPONSE

*Vianne Timmons*

This essay highlights an important global issue: HIV/AIDS. When we look at the international figures on the prevalence of this disease, it is frightening. Vulnerable populations are often viewed as disposable and do not get the services or support they need to combat this disease. Claudia Mitchell discusses the importance of educating teachers, and through them, Canadian youth about HIV/AIDS.

It is important when reading Claudia's essay that you, as teachers, think about your social responsibility to our youth. Claudia gives us ways to incorporate this important topic into teaching our youth, especially through literature. These practical suggestions are designed to connect with youth using technology and creativity. She highlights the value of viewing youth as "knowledge producers." She points out that we need to involve youth in creating and producing messages if we want to connect with youth.

Her work with beginning teachers highlights the many issues teachers face when exploring issues such as HIV/AIDS in other countries. Whose voice is valued and privileged? What right do Canadian teachers have to use literature from other countries and discuss issues that are adversely affecting the developing world? My response to these questions is to ask, what right do Canadian teachers have not to explore issues of developing countries, expose children to literature from other countries, and ensure our children are aware that many issues are local ones and not just relevant to international settings? This is the obligation of teachers.

Claudia stresses that action is important and uses the example of her preservice class collecting school supplies for South Africa. Connecting teachers and students to global social justice issues is imperative. We live in a global context where children are exposed to unbelievable amounts of information and can easily become desensitized to vital social issues. We, as teacher educators, need to provide opportunities for preservice teachers to learn about social justice issues in a global context and explore how to engage children and youth in this learning.

This generation has been raised with an awareness of discrimination, inequalities, and injustice. But they usually do not have the opportunity to connect this to their lives and communities and take action. They will rise to this opportunity, if presented, and preservice teachers can transform their lives through this learning. Students can learn how they can make a difference, leave a footprint, locally, regionally, nationally, and internationally. We need to facilitate this learning.

Claudia has given us a challenge. We need to embrace this challenge and be creative ourselves if we want our graduates to be creative in our schools. This is a wonderful way to engage our students and role model for them how to enable "knowledge producers."

# Overcoming Barriers to Inclusivity

## Preparing Preservice Teachers for Diversity

*Vianne Timmons*

Teacher education is a field containing significant pressures in curriculum, practicum design and in the roles and relationships with schools. This essay will explore inclusive practices and teacher education, a vital area of social justice. Inclusive education is a relatively new field that became relevant in developed countries in the 1980s and more recently in developing countries.

The history of educating children with disabilities has been one of exclusion, institutionalization, and segregation. Through parent and organization advocacy, human rights activists, and statements from international organizations, the landscape has changed. Two key international declarations have been the Salamanca Statement (1994) and more recently the UN Convention on the Rights of Persons with Disabilities in 2006. The Salamanca Statement identified inclusive education as the means to achieve Education for All (EFA). Ninety-two countries and twenty-five international organizations signed this important declaration. Over 100 countries have signed the UN Convention, which states in article 24:

In realizing this right, States Parties shall ensure:

(a) That persons with disabilities are not excluded from the general education system on the basis of disability, and that children with disabilities are not excluded from free and compulsory primary and secondary education on the basis of disability;
(b) That persons with disabilities can access an inclusive, quality, free primary and secondary education on an equal basis with others in the communities in which they live;
(c) Reasonable accommodation of the individual's requirements;
(d) That persons with disabilities receive the support required, within the general education system, to facilitate their effective education;
(e) That effective individualized support measures are provided in environments that maximize academic and social development, consistent with the goal of full inclusion.

These statements have important implications for teacher education internationally. To prepare teachers for inclusive classrooms requires changes in curriculum, expertise, and practicum placements. We need to prepare teachers adequately to ensure that this notion of education for all is realized.

There is no standard approach in teacher education to prepare teachers to teach children with exceptional needs. In Canada, educators estimate that about 15 percent of students have special learning needs (Timmons, 2006). Some universities, in their teacher education programs, offer elective courses on diversity, while others have the subject as a core component of their curriculum. Lupart et al. (2004) highlight the need for teachers and administrators to be better prepared to meet the needs of diverse students in today's classrooms. However, preparing teachers for an inclusive classroom is a complex endeavour.

One of the first challenges is the question, who is a diverse learner? There are learners with different abilities, religions, races, genders, and sexual orientations in our classrooms. Some universities teach a categorization approach to teaching diverse learners. They provide curriculum that prepares teachers to teach children with Down's syndrome, English as a Second Language, behavioral difficulty, and other specific categories. The difficulty with this approach is the sheer number of categories. For example, in Alberta, Canada, there were 56 students in 1950 identified with special learning needs as compared to 77,703 in 2002 (Lupart et al., 2004). Category-based approaches to teaching preservice teachers about disability issues reinforce the idea that children are and should be labelled to be taught effectively. They also perpetuate the stereotypes of the labelled children and do not focus the preservice teacher on essential areas, such as learning needs, attitudes, and different approaches to teaching all children.

As global mobility becomes more commonplace, the world is becoming increasingly multicultural, especially in developed countries. Sapon-Shevin and Zollers (1999) highlight the emerging connotations of the word *inclusion*, as it incorporates issues beyond culture and disability and also includes poverty. The researchers note that changes in teacher education ought to encompass philosophy, pedagogy, and advocacy, along with curriculum. They indicate that there has only been a traditional approach to meeting this challenge, offering discrete courses such as multicultural education and/or special education. Again specific courses serve a limited purpose as they typically are survey courses with significant breadth and little depth.

The solution is elusive. The demands on teacher education curriculum is significant and includes—literacy, numeracy, technology, social studies, science, art, health, child development, social justice, school parental relations, leadership, and other topics—which are each important but impossible to cover here. The traditional training of special education teachers has changed to ensure that this education be incorporated into regular teacher education programs and often through postgraduate programs.

One of the challenges teachers face as they are educated to teach in an inclusive classroom is that many did not graduate from a system that was inclusive. They have few if any experiences or models they can draw on. They are forced to create classrooms that they have only read about rather than ones they have experienced. Even in their practicum experiences, they may have a limited exposure to inclusive practices. The educational system has a variable approach to inclusive classrooms, with many children still educated in segregated classrooms, especially at the middle and secondary level, and pulled out for one-on-one work or remediation at the elementary level. When these new teachers graduate and enter the teaching profession, they have few role models to help them implement inclusive practices in their classrooms.

Jordan and Stanovich (2004) identified characteristics of teachers that are useful for incorporating inclusionary practices into teaching. These include believing that educating children with special needs is their responsibility, teacher efficacy, and inclusionary practices being established at their school. In teacher education programs, preservice teachers need an opportunity to explore their beliefs and biases. If teacher educators do not present curriculum that is infused with inclusionary practices, it will be challenging for new teachers to recognize their responsibility to include all learners.

The research on teacher education (Nevin et al., 2007) highlights that beliefs and attitudes about inclusion and students with special needs can change if there are opportunities for successful interaction with people with disabilities. This research presents powerful evidence that should guide practicum planning for preservice teachers. There should be opportunities throughout the teacher education program to interact and form relationships with students from different backgrounds and abilities. Often practicum placements are secured for students based on which teachers will take them; this does not ensure that we are graduating competent teachers who believe in promoting inclusive practices in their classrooms. Mayhew and Grunwald's research (2006) points out that university professors who support issues such as affirmative action are more likely to incorporate diversity-related content into their teaching. As with classroom teachers, the attitudes and beliefs of teacher educators are critical to the transformation of the attitudes of their students.

The educational system also often works against promoting inclusive practices. There is a significant trend toward standardized testing and increased standards in schools. We have seen schools ranked based on the results of these standardized tests, with parents choosing schools and schools selecting students based on these results. New teachers are often under pressure to ensure that their classes perform well on these tests, while individualized instruction, differentiated teaching, or teaching outside the curriculum is often discouraged. A significant disconnect then occurs between their teacher education programs and the realities of the system.

Another area of concern is the lack of diversity among teachers (Finley, 2000). Classrooms are filled with students of different races, cultures, genders and abilities, and teachers are predominately white, female middle-class and monolingual. They often have a limited personal experience with interracial and intercultural interactions and do not know firsthand what it is like to live with a learning difficulty. Mayhew and Grunwald (2006), in examining factors that contribute to university faculty incorporating diversity-related content into their teaching, found that professors of different races were more likely to incorporate diversity-related content into their teaching than white professors.

To encourage teachers to incorporate inclusive practices, especially those from the dominant race and culture, experiences in their education programs that connect them with diverse students in their classrooms are needed. Finley (2000) stresses the need to integrate multicultural perspectives into the content and structures of teacher education programs. The same will need to happen in the field of disability, all courses should be infused with the knowledge and understanding to empower teachers to teach subjects such as math and language arts to all learners. This requires teacher educators to be knowledgeable about more than the content of the subject area.

Throughout the first postsecondary education degree, teacher educators are prepared in one subject area or content area, such as history or science. Their focus as they enter teacher education is to transform that content knowledge to learner knowledge. The content becomes the vehicle to teach preservice teachers about learning and hopefully diversity is embedded in all we do. Becoming familiar with the field of diversity and inclusion can be a steep learning curve for many teacher educators who have not formally studied these fields. It is incumbent upon them to work with colleagues and ensure that curriculum areas are addressing inclusionary practices.

Jordon and Stanovich (2004) found in their work that teachers who implement successful inclusive practices become teachers who advocate and support inclusion. Schools need support systems in place to ensure teachers can experiment and try new methodologies that focus on supporting all children. These schools then are ideal for practicum placements for preservice teachers. There is good reason for teacher education programs to promote inclusive practice in schools, as it leads to better practices for our preservice teachers to model.

Recent research (Hawkins, 2007) connects the improved academic performance of students to inclusionary practices. Williams (2002) demonstrates that classrooms with heterogeneous-ability-grouped children have an overall greater academic achievement than homogeneous-ability-grouped children. This type of research needs to be incorporated into teacher education practices, since our ultimate goal is to increase student success in our schools. More research that assesses the academic achievement of all students in inclusive classrooms is required. This research is critical as inclusive practices are advocated internationally. The process of moving toward inclusive settings should be documented and evaluated in a systematic ongoing way.

Kabeer (2000) questions whether the concept of inclusive practice, which originated in developed countries, is appropriate for developing countries. With more than one hundred countries signing on to the UN Convention, inclusive education is now a global educational trend. Many countries, such as South Africa, have enabling legislation to ensure that inclusive placements are the norm for all children. The challenge in many countries is to develop teacher education programs that support such school legislation.

Many schools in developing countries are under-resourced, understaffed, and challenged in providing education to children. In particular, children with special needs are often totally excluded from the educational, economic, and social system. They are kept at home, still often hidden. On a recent trip to Sri Lanka, this author visited rural communities where children with special needs were kept at home, and families were embarrassed to take their children out into the community due to a lack of understanding and perceived ridicule.

In spite of this situation in developing countries, there are examples where advocates make notable gains in inclusive practices. The National Resource Centre for Inclusion in Mumbai, India, has worked diligently to educate schools and have children with special needs accepted and supported. Dyson and Zhang (2004), in a comparative study on teachers' attitudes toward inclusion in Canada and China, found Chinese teachers had a positive attitude toward inclusion and children's well-being. Teacher education programs can learn from how different countries promote inclusive practices in their own programming.

It is at the teacher education level that we can begin to influence teachers' attitudes and beliefs toward children from different backgrounds, cultures and abilities. This will require several support systems to be in place. To begin with, the infusion of curriculum with diverse information to support teachers in implementing inclusive practices into their teaching is needed. Correspondingly, carefully selected and researched practicum placements that promote inclusion are necessary. In addition, professional development with schools to support them in moving toward inclusive practices must be continually incorporated. Finally, attention must be paid to ensure preservice teachers spend time with children with different abilities and backgrounds in some capacity in the teacher education program.

With the pressures on teachers to teach more math and reading, prepare children for standardized tests, deal with bullying in schools, complete increased paperwork, and to continually upgrade their knowledge and skills, focusing on inclusionary practices could easily drop to the bottom of the priority list. Porath and Jordan state that "we are presently at a crossroad in educating students in all disciplines. . . Students and teachers find themselves grappling with old experiences and conceptions of education. Many cling to the model of knowledge delivery as the best way to educate" (2004, p. 57). Inclusive practices are not about the transmission of knowledge. They are about involving children, working with their strengths, participating in active learning and peer interaction, and using differentiated curriculum. Hutchinson (2004) found that preservice teachers, who viewed teaching as interactive and not merely the transmission of knowledge, paid attention to students' individual differences and were open to inclusive practices. Inclusive practice has the potential to transform our classrooms, and allows for vibrant, efficient learning communities that educate all children to emerge.

Lenski et al. (2005) stated that textbook coursework in multicultural education has not prepared teachers to work with children from diverse cultures. If such coursework is not effective, then other options must be explored, such as carefully crafted practicum options and infusions into the curriculum. Preservice teachers must become conscious of the importance of attitudes and bias and the only way that will happen is if teacher educators become conscious of their own bias and the impact of their attitudes. Preparing teachers for inclusive settings is not only a curriculum issue but also a cultural issue. Time must be committed to explore personal cultural beliefs and beliefs about ability, and also to reflect on how these attitudes and beliefs affect our teaching.

# RESPONSE

## *Claudia Mitchell*

Vianne Timmons in her essay offers a series of critical challenges to those of us who are interested in preservice teacher education and are concerned that new teachers receive the support they need to ensure quality education for all. As she points out, global policies and strategies that ensure governments have appropriate frameworks within which to act are at the heart of much of this work. However, as she highlights, the gap between policy and action is key. The two most difficult (and interrelated) questions that her essay poses pertain to (1) what inclusion actually means (and how do we avoid the compartmentalization of inclusivity into discrete issues?), and (2) how do teachers themselves (regardless of whether they are preservice or in-service) locate themselves within issues of social justice broadly and within inclusive education specifically? As Timmons observes, the majority of teachers, certainly in the North American context are female, white, and more commonly middle-class.

Obviously there are no easy answers, but perhaps a curriculum for teacher education that pays heed to a "starting-with-ourselves" approach privileging self-study would be an excellent entry point. (See, for example, the work of Pithouse, 2007; Loughran et al., 2004; Hamilton, 1998; Mitchell, Weber & Pithouse, in press; Mitchell & Weber, 2005.) As this work suggests, the "ourselves" includes teacher educators along with preservice teachers. We might look to some of the work in countries such as South Africa that have not had the luxury of several decades to try to "get it right" but, nonetheless, through fairly recent legislation such as White Paper 6 have been moving quickly to implement policies around inclusive education that call attention to the impact of poverty and HIV and AIDS on learners. (Mitchell, De Lange & Nguyen, in press). Indeed, as the papers attest in a special issue of the *International Journal of Inclusive Education* on the impact of HIV and AIDS on education in South Africa, a broad and inclusive definition of inclusive education has to be the starting point (Mitchell, Moletsane & De Lange, 2007. This work takes us to many new questions, but the two I want to end with are the first two questions we invite the reader to consider below.

# We invite the reader to consider the following questions:

1. To what extent are teacher education faculties prepared to take on a rigorous approach to self-study?

2. Recognizing the success of new perspectives being explored elsewhere, what might faculties of education in North America do to engage more effectively in South-North dialogue with international partners such as Ministries of Education and Faculties of Education in universities in China and South Africa?

3. What potential issues might teachers face in developing curriculum about HIV/AIDS in high schools?

4. How can we foster a greater understanding and awareness of the impact of HIV/AIDS in elementary students?

THEME 5

# Imagining Sustainable Futures for the Work of Teachers

CONTRIBUTING AUTHORS

Anne M. Phelan

James Trier

# A New Thing in an Old World?

## Instrumentalism, Teacher Education, and Responsibility

*Anne M. Phelan*

"And what is the use of use?" (Arendt, 1998, p. 154)

### Introduction

A range of policies in the 1980s and 1990s in North America and Europe has progressively contributed to reducing education and teacher education to the production of pre-determined outcomes (Furlong et al., 2000). The definition of teacher competences; the establishment of teaching standards by "Colleges of Teachers"; the introduction of licensed and certified teacher schemes; the creation of prescriptive, outcome-based curricula; and systems of accountability through standardized testing are obvious examples of such reductionism (Smyth & Shacklock, 1998; Phelan, 1996). According to some, professional autonomy is being seriously curtailed. In an effort to secure and protect some vestige of autonomy, prominent researchers (of teaching and teacher education) have become preoccupied with matters of *justification* (delineation of the knowledge base for teaching and teacher education), *legitimation* (assertion of the need for university-based teacher education), and *recognition* of teaching as a state-of-the-art profession. While the political necessity of such moves might be obvious, the upshot is these preoccupations entangle teaching and teacher education in the very logic of utility (instrumental reasoning/means-end thinking) that characterizes much of contemporary policy. By instrumental reasoning I mean, "that mode of thinking that tries to answer the question of how we can reach an end rather than why that end is what we should aim for at all" (O'Byrne, 2005, p. 396).

In this essay, I identify the prevalence of means-ends thinking in educational thought and practice. I argue that the expansion of instrumental thinking constricts the radical possibilities of teaching and teacher education as democratic action. I propose that teacher education might be better served by research that engages the aporetic condition of teacher education as a site of possibility.

## The Instrumentalist Coin

On September 5, 2006, the first day back at school for many children in British Columbia, newspapers across Canada covered "President [Bush]'s National Strategy for Combating Terrorism." In a presentation made to the Military Officers Association of America, President Bush said:

> [W]e're engaged in a global war against an enemy that threatens all civilized nations. And today the civilized world stands together to defend our freedom; we stand together to defeat the terrorists; and we're working to secure the peace for generations to come . . . Our strategy for combating terrorism has five basic elements . . . to stay on the offense . . . (*President discusses global war on terror*, 2006)

In reading this text, one can easily be seduced by simplistic and rigid dichotomies—good and evil, virtuous and vicious. One of the deepest strains in popular culture is the simplistic way that we divide the world into good guys and bad guys. We demonize our enemies and in quasi-religious talk speak of the "evil" ones to be eliminated. There is no compromise or diplomacy, no time for judgment, judicious discrimination, and negotiation (Bernstein, 2007). Media coverage of education is a case in point; consider the following news story in the *Montreal Gazette*.

> Thrown into a tough secondary school during her teacher training, Melanie Bertrand started questioning her career choice. "There were fights, the cops were constantly there—it was mind-boggling," Bertrand said. "The kids, they didn't want to be there." Bertrand had a starkly different experience at another school, which convinced her to stay the course. "You don't have to discipline these kids, they actually ask for more work," she said of her stint at the tony, private Lower Canada College in N.D.G. Since the early 1990s, Quebec universities with teacher-training programs have added courses in classroom management and beefed up in-class training . . . Bertrand wishes she had even more training in classroom management. "We were never taught to deal with the students, the unruly and unmanageable ones," she says." (Dougherty, 2006)

The virtuous and the vicious reappear in the guise of private and public school attendees. Not unlike a commander-in-chief, the risk-conscious teacher, supervisor of unruly bodies, must be alert to potential dangers (McWilliam, 2008). To teach in "tough" schools, the teacher must be "trained" in the scrutiny of her students. "In-class training" must be "beefed up" to produce a teacher with an adaptable disposition toward the challenges of public school life (Phelan & Sumsion, 2008). Caught in a cycle of disillusionment with a troubled world and nostalgia for a world in which nations and children are civilized, we enter political and educational discourses of safety/risk, order/disorder, normal/abnormal, and perpetrator/redeemer. In an era of risk consciousness, coldly rational calculation is now the logic for thinking about social and organizational good (McWilliam, 2008).

Nostalgia for a trouble-free world is not limited to right-wing ideologues, however. Attempts to reclaim "a robust, comprehensive, and unitary public sphere" that can "gather us together" around shared purposes are central to many communitarians and participatory democrats for whom democracy has been undercut by the emergence of the "national security state" and the rendering meaningless of the term *citizen* (Villa, 1997, p. 199). Claiming that alienation from one another is the source of the difficulty, educators, in this vein, devise curricula for social responsibility (British Columbia Ministry of Education, 2008) or mutual understanding (see Phelan, 2001, on teacher education in Northern Ireland), conspire to build communities of practice in educational settings, and critique the economic logic that drives institutional decision-making. Left-of-centre appeals to intersubjectivity, dialogue, and democracy are seductive, but Hannah Arendt cautions us, "the chances that tomorrow will be like yesterday are always overwhelming" (Levinson, 2001, p. 14).

Attempts to recover or secure particular ends may reflect a regression to what Dewey called "the quest for certainty" and Hilary Putnam calls the "craving for absolutes" (Bernstein, 2007, p. 2). Recovery and security are two sides of the same coin of a generalized instrumentalism that reduces politics and education to anthropocentric projects of calculation, strategy, and human mastery. Educators and political leaders lose an appreciation for "the distinction between utility and meaningfulness . . . between 'in order to' and 'for the sake of'" (Arendt, 1998, p. 157). Politics and education appear devoid of any intrinsic or independent value. Sarah Dougherty's report in the *Montreal Gazette* is endemic of such a process reality wherein larger questions of what and why are usurped by how (Arendt, 1998). There is no deliberation about educational purposes, no consideration of authority in teaching, no apparent concern for the manner in which schools shape and are shaped by social inequities, no reference to the complex responsibility of the teacher and teacher educators toward the life of children and for the continuance of the world (Phelan & Sumsion, 2008). When did (teacher) education become so small (Smits, 2008)?

## Instrumentalism and the Teaching-Learning Trap

The educational enterprise has long been characterized by discussions of how we are to secure (or recover) particular ends. Possessed by instrumental thinking, educators educate, Pinar (2004) writes, *in order to* produce social justice, achievement scores, or psycho-social outcomes. Tracing the educational preoccupation with mastery of the world to Edward L. Thorndike's social engineering, Pinar continues,

> Social engineering, simply called "human engineering" by Edward L. Thorndike, appears to assume that education is like a complex automobile engine: if only we make the right adjustments—in teaching, in learning, in assessment—it will hum, and transport us to our destination, the promised land of high test scores, or for many of us on the educational Left, a truly democratic society. (Pinar, 2004, p. 1)

Pinar's discussion returns us to an era when the attentional economy of the masses was a central concern. William James' emphasis on the autonomy of attention ("each of us literally chooses, by his ways of attending to things, what sort of a universe he shall appear to himself to inhabit" [in Pinar, 2004, p. 7]) occurred when technologies and institutions, including the school, were being designed to command the attention of mass populations. Apparently, James is contradicting the influential work of another writer (William B. Carpenter) done in the 1870s in which attention is described as an element of subjectivity to be externally shaped and controlled.

> It is the aim of the Teacher to fix the attention of the Pupil upon objects which may have in themselves little or no attraction for it . . . The habit of attention, at first purely automatic, gradually becomes, by judicious training, in great degree amenable to the Will of the Teacher, who encourages it by the suggestion of appropriate moves, whilst taking care not to overstrain the child's mind by too long dwelling upon one object. (Carpenter, 1886, in Pinar, 2004, p. 7)

Pedagogical regulation paralleled other disciplinary forms of self-regulation and self-control in the 19th century. As a result, Pinar argues, the notion of study was lost as was the notion of teachers inciting a passion for study, and we have instead "learning" tied tightly, of course, to assessment and instruction. Even "curriculum"—presumably the content of learning—mutates to a means to the end that is assessment.

One result of this is that teaching became instrumental to learning. Once learning described what a person accomplished as a result of serious study, Pinar writes, now learning is seen as a consequence of teaching. "Concomitantly, learning limits study to what is taught, it performs the dirty work of accountability, that covers for the closure of academic—intellectual—

freedom in contemporary classrooms" (Pinar, 2004, p. 8). While the author acknowledges that teaching can be theorized and practiced in fascinating, even magical ways, as the pedagogy of Ted Aoki suggests, he asks: "Does not the very concept tempt us to think we can at a minimum, influence, or more optimistically (or is it arrogantly?) produce, certain effects or consequences?" (p. 11).

Disciplinary attention to instruction or teaching or pedagogy as the production of certain consequences sets intellectual and political traps for the teacher.

> Power and responsibility accompany the command of attention. It becomes the teacher upon whom the student depends in order to learn: that is the intellectual trap. And it is the teacher who becomes responsible for student learning: that is the political trap. What the conjunctive relationship between curriculum and teaching . . . . invites, then, is an inflation of the claims and liabilities of the teacher (intellectual/academic education, psycho-social reconstruction, or workplace utility) that deludes parents and politicians (not to mention students and teachers) that the locus of responsibility—the very site of education—is the teacher, not the student (Pinar, 2004, pp. 11–12).

The inflation of claims and liabilities of the teacher (as a means to the end of learning) has also driven several decades of educational research.

## Instrumentalism and the Snare of Teacher Education Research

There are three classic routes by which educational research has tried to gain authority over and influence the practice of teachers (Pearson, 2005). First, rational empirical approaches reflect the operative principle "know the truth and the truth shall make you free." The operative metaphor is "sowing the seeds of knowledge for a rich harvest of improved practice" (p. 3). The theory of action implied in such accounts of the impact of research on practice and policy is straightforward. The hope is that teachers are exposed to such research via educational journals, books, and conferences. In normative re-educative approaches, the assumption is that research needs a little nudge, and so staff developers are charged with negotiating change at the local level. Such approaches also include teacher research groups and school- and district-based communities of inquiry. Finally, power-coercive approaches are evident when governments and other institutional bodies coerce teachers to change when using laws, court rulings, and legislative or executive mandates as the primary policy levers (Pearson, 2005). The advent of teaching standards in Alberta, Ontario, and British Columbia that attempt to shape teacher preparation and evaluation priorities is one such example.

Similarly, the history of teacher education as a field of study seems largely connected, in the United States and the United Kingdom at least, to a confluence of events and reports asserting that *teachers are failing* and schools are in trouble. The critique of teacher education is never too far from the wake of such reports: lack of intellectual rigour, selectivity standards, structural arrangements, research base, failure to achieve positive results in schools and classrooms—ending in calls for program reform and more sharply focused research. Consider, for example, the questions that have driven research in teacher education since the 1950s (Cochran-Smith & Fries, 2006):

1. How do we produce effective behaviours in prospective teachers so that program and policy decisions can be empirically based? (1950s–1980s)
2. What should teachers learn and be able to do? (1980s–2000s)
3. Does teacher education make a difference? (2000–present)

A recent news report illustrates the centrality of "teacher performance" in conversations about education in Asia and Australia:

> Education administrators throughout Asia and Australia agree that the quality of teachers and teaching needs improvement but are still unsure how performance can be improved, according to the Director of the South East Asian Ministers' of Education Organization (SEAMEO), Dr. Edilberto de Jesus. Dr. de Jesus, who was previously the Philippines' minister in charge of education, will be discussing the role of teacher education in improving teaching performance at the inaugural 'Training Tomorrows' Teachers' forum to be held at the University of Melbourne next week, commencing Monday 4 June. "Everyone agrees that teachers need help so that they can do their jobs better, but it is not so easy to determine just exactly what their job is or how to help improve their performance," says Dr. de Jesus. (*University of Melbourne News*, 2007)

Consistently, prominent researchers (of teaching and teacher education) seem preoccupied with matters of *justification* (delineation of knowledge base for teaching and teacher education), *legitimation* (assertion of the need for university-based teacher education) and *recognition* (teacher autonomy). While understandable and to some degree necessary in a climate hostile to education and educators, the danger is that such language and preoccupations entangle teaching and teacher education in a logic of utility (instrumental reasoning) that risks reducing both to a means to some end.

Linda Darling-Hammond and John Bransford's 2005 edited collection, *Preparing Teachers for a Changing World: What Teachers Should Learn and Be Able to Do*, may be a case in point. The text, sponsored by the National Academy of Education, attempts to review research and theory in a range of knowledge domains including "Teaching Subject Matter" (Chapter 6), "Teaching Diverse Learners" (Chapter 7), "Assessment" (Chapter 8), and "Classroom Management" (Chapter 9). The major impetus of this body of work is the promotion of teaching as a state-of-the-art profession—knowledge-based, deliberate, and rational, with knowledgeable teachers and reflective curriculum leaders. The intent is that curriculum renewal in teacher education might be guided accordingly.

In the urgency to address perceived challenges or solve perceived problems, Darling-Hammond and Bransford seem to be curiously uncritical about the very sense of normativity they deploy (Butler, 2002). For the question, "What are we to do in/with teacher education?" presupposes "that the 'we' has been formed and that it is known, that its action is possible, and the field in which it might act is delimited. But if those very formations and delimitations have normative consequences, then it will be necessary to ask after the values that set the stage for action" (Butler, 2002, p. 215).

First, induced by neo-liberal policies to assert a professional knowledge base for teaching and teacher education, such a compendium of research may end up denying the plurality that exists among researchers by collapsing disparate perspectives into unanimity, forcing premature closure. Particulars are devoured by generalities as pattern is mistaken for meaning. Claiming to operate in the public interest radically undermines the possibility of a common world, a public sphere where the project of education, and teacher education, must always raise deeply controversial and contested questions about the proper direction of human flourishing (Coulter, 2006).

Second, there is the implication that teacher education based on theory and research guarantees effective teaching and subsequently, student achievement. When human action (the education of teachers in this case) is framed as a form of fabrication or production (teachers as assessors or classroom managers), the researchers are in danger of reverting to the age-old attempt to escape the fragility, unpredictability, and frustration of action. All action in the world between humans is consequential, affecting and altering the course of events (Arendt, 1998). Practical judgments of teachers or teacher educators are not authorized by certainties but can only propose versions of them (Wingrove, 2007). Seeking to emphasize the presentness of action, Hannah Arendt (1998) tried to guard against the faith of modern ideologies in the future consequences of present means.

Third, it is this very unpredictability of action that allows faith in the power of educators to break away from the status quo, to start something new, to give expression to what others take to be impossible dreams and hopes. Could teachers or teacher educators not be people with a "revolutionary spirit," who can keep alive the utopian moment in thinking that refuses to accept what presently exists as the measure of all reality? Could there be more to teaching than the exercise of adaptive expertise (Darling-Hammond & Bransford, 2005)? In summary, research that seeks to secure professionalism in this manner is in danger of denying plurality and refusing the possibility of action; in promoting paternalism, it constricts freedom. Ironically, the researchers may lead us away from that which they hoped to secure—professional autonomy. Research carried out in the name of justice can be unjust, after all (Lovelie, 2007).

None of this suggests, however, that teacher education can never be understood as *poiesis* or production, including decisions about what teachers should learn and organizing so that they might learn what are deemed desirable knowledge, skills, or dispositions, setting up a program, evaluating. To think solely in these terms, however policy driven or resistant, is to neglect teaching and teacher education as forms of praxis.

> *Praxis* is concerned with ethical action and the ultimate end of *praxis* is to act well, to lead a good and worthwhile life, an activity that inevitably involves relationships with other people and the intertwining of ends and means. (Coulter et al., 2007)

Not unlike teachers, teacher educators are responsible for helping teacher candidates discover their own worthwhile lives by helping them acquire the requisite knowledge, skills and dispositions or virtues to succeed in teaching. Not unlike teachers, teacher educators are responsible for discovering the means and ends in context, in particular relationships (Coulter et al., 2007). Lovelie (2007) writes:

> When ends and means are set, our responsibilities are accordingly set and circumscribed. The procedures for making validity claims good, the technicisms of legitimate action both extend and curb our democratic responsibilities. The same paradox befalls teaching when . . . virtues harden into set habits. (p. 18)

The crux of texts such as *Preparing Teachers for a Changing World* is that responsible teacher education may just take the responsibility out of teacher education.

## Thinking Responsibly in Teacher Education Research

Not unlike teachers, researchers are perennially caught between the unconditional, ethical impulse to act for the sake of some "good," and the conditional adaptation of this impulse to historically available institutional means for pursuing that "good" (Brennan & Zipin, 2008). In the contemporary political climate of United States, the institutional means for Darling-Hammond and colleagues is that of producing a so-called scientific evidence base to justify teacher professionalism and university-based teacher education. The language of *in order to* usurps that of *for the sake of*. Researchers thus find themselves caught.

> That is not easy. It is even impossible to conceive of a responsibility that consists in being responsible for *two* laws, or that consists in responding to two contradictory injunctions. No doubt. But there is no responsibility that is not the experience and experiment of the impossible. (Derrida, 1992, p. 44–5)

Research is like teaching and teacher education in this regard: it is entangled in an ethical *aporia*, or unresolvable perplexity (Derrida, 2001). Without acknowledging this perplexity, researchers may simply produce "comfort texts" that try to provide all the necessary consolations to policy makers and practitioners (Lather, 1997). An acknowledgment of ethical aporia, on the other hand, may invite an opportunity to think differently, in a materially difficult way, about "teaching" and "teacher education." Arendt may be instructive here.

Thinking, for Arendt, is not about deducing, inducing, and drawing conclusions whose logical rules of non-contradiction and inner consistency can be learned once and for all and then need only to be applied. Raising questions without providing neat answers was a key purpose in thinking. She wrote that she did not feel duty bound to solve the difficulties her thinking created. Thinking, for her, was a battleground, a fighting experience that can be won only through practice, through exercises. Kohn (2006) writes,

> These (exercises) do not contain prescriptions on what to think and or which truths to hold. Least of all, do they intend to retie the broken thread of tradition or to invent some newfangled surrogates with which to fill the gap between past and future ... the problem of truth is kept in abeyance; the concern is solely to move in this gap—the only region perhaps where truth eventually will appear. (p. xiv)

Arendt (2006) seemed to reverse the established relationship between experience and thought. She refers to Kafka, who, in her view, took the bare minimum of experience and created a kind of thought-landscape that harbored all the riches, varieties, and dramatic elements characteristic of "real" life (Kohn, 2006). Thinking with Kafka and Arendt, alongside Melanie Bertrand, what questions might her experience evoke/provoke? Given our educational legacy, our first impulse may be to ask what must Melanie know and be able to do? However, Arendt, along with many postmodern writers such as Derrida, Butler, and Foucault, urges us to curb our impatience to resolve matters and to keep the avenues of dialogue open.

What if, in a hesitant pause, researchers wondered about the (im)possibility of hospitality toward the newcomer to the profession, the complications of friendship in teaching and learning, experience as both gift and curse, teacher learning as a loss of truth and self as much as an assurance of self and identity, teacher knowledge as site of hope and despair (Lovelie, 2007)? What if researchers focused on language, asking in Socratic style, what do we mean when we say . . . ? In so doing, researchers might immerse themselves in the unresolvable perplexity of being at once guardians of an idea of "teacher" but also bound by the responsibility of an intellectual to open the notion of "teacher" to the difference that which is not, never was, and may never be "teacher."

None of this means that research such as that conducted by Darling-Hammond and colleagues must end—rather it calls for a reflection that widens the field of insight in teacher education. It does mean, however, that learning to live with unease, Lather (2004) writes, always feeling a bit lost in the service of unlocking thinking, opens ourselves up to "intellectual bewilderment" (p. 8). Researchers who work in this manner refuse to be seduced by clarity or common sense while at the same time attempting to be understood. They risk unrecognizability and unintelligibility as "researchers" while still attempting to appear "relevant." They accept the terms of what has been/is while acting in ways that might renew those terms. While starting in existing states of affairs is necessary, researchers must eschew the tools and technicisms of instrumentalism, for the sake of teacher education that invites plurality of thought, which welcomes the natality of action, and accepts the fragility of both.

Can our work in teacher education preserve thought and action? Can research proceed "without a project" (O'Byrne, 2005)? Is teacher education "something that is capable of surprising itself, something interested in risking itself?" (Britzman, 1998, p 58). Could it be a new thing in an old world (Arendt, 2006)?

# RESPONSE

## James Trier

The main object of critique in Phelan's essay is "instrumental reasoning," which she defines as a form of reasoning that ignores questions of *why* something should be done and instead seeks to answer *how* something should be done. Most public school teachers experience the everyday effects of the many forms of the instrumental (means/end) reasoning that Phelan describes. For example, most teachers no longer bother to seriously discuss (in, say, faculty meetings or teacher workdays) the reasons why they must attempt to prepare their students for the inevitable standardized testing that will take place. Instead, most teachers have resigned themselves to this fact of testing and consequently set aside a block of time a few weeks before the test in order to put their students through the paces of preparing for the test.

Along with public school teachers (and administrators), most teacher educators working in schools of education also find themselves entangled in discourses shaped in large part by one or another form of instrumental reasoning. For example, many schools of education undergo every few years or so a review by some accreditation body, such as NCATE (National Council for Accreditation of Teacher Education). And to prepare for an NCATE review, teacher educators are forced to provide a plethora of tedious data that demonstrates that preservice teachers have been on the receiving end of the proper pedagogical ministrations for acquiring the skills, knowledge, and dispositions that NCATE (not the teacher educators themselves) has determined must be acquired to become a licensed teacher.

Phelan's essay provides teacher educators and teachers with a powerful critique of instrumental reasoning, a critique that indeed opens up (in her words) "an opportunity to think differently, in a materially difficult way, about 'teaching' and 'teacher education.'" And though I agree with much of what Phelan articulates and argues about instrumental reasoning, I also found myself not agreeing with a few things.

One thing occurs when (drawing on the writing of Pinar, 2004) Phelan asserts, "Possessed by instrumental reasoning, educators educate . . . *in order to* produce social justice, achievement scores, or psycho-social outcomes." For me, Phelan's (and Pinar's) inclusion of "social justice" with "achievement scores" is a conflation of two very different things. Against such a conflation, I would argue that an educator working toward the end—yes, I have said it: toward an end—of social justice will likely be working *against* the very form of instrumental reasoning that has tangled, ensnared, trapped, and possessed educators into discourses of standardized testing.

Another thing I wondered about was what I interpret to be a problematic assumption that Phelan seems to make. On my reading (and I could very well be missing something), Phelan seems to assume that Education (writ large) is currently dominated by discourses of instrumental reasoning, therefore we (teachers and teacher educators) *necessarily* end up feeling *only* caught up, trapped, entangled, possessed by, and ensnared within a matrix of means/end discourses. I do not find in her argument any acknowledgment that many teachers and teacher educators are already engaging in the very kind of "praxis" that Phelan calls for us to engage in. In other words, is it not quite possible that teachers and teacher educators work *simultaneously* within and yet also challenge and subvert discourses of instrumental reason?

# Subversive Engagements in Teacher Education

## *James Trier*

In *Teaching as a Subversive Activity*, Neil Postman and Charles Weingartner (1969) presented an argument that rests upon an opposition between two radically different forms of education. The inferior form was what the authors called "the old education," which referred not to some passing or defunct education but to the still dominant and pervasive education practices and policies at the time. The authors described this "old education" as consisting of millions of "conventional" teachers perpetrating unimaginative, routine, teacher-centered practices that produced uncritical, unimaginative, obedient students who lacked the strategies to survive in the complex, challenging adult world toward which they were inevitably headed. People forced to endure the old education "come out as passive, acquiescent, dogmatic, intolerant, authoritarian, inflexible, conservative personalities who desperately need to resist change in an effort to keep their illusion of certainty intact" (p. 217).

For Postman and Weingartner, this form of education had to be subverted because it posed a grave threat to the survival of both the students who were subjected to it and to our society as a whole. To subvert this threat, the authors called for a "new education" whose main purpose would be

> the development of a new kind of person, one who—as a result of internalizing a different series of concepts—is an actively inquiring, flexible, creative, innovative, liberal personality who can face uncertainty and ambiguity without disorientation, who can formulate viable new meanings to meet changes in the environment which threaten individual and mutual survival. (p. 218)

For the new education to come about, a new kind of teacher first had to appear. Though Postman and Weingartner acknowledged that there were indeed some public school teachers already engaging in the new education at the time, they believed that "the major source of teachers for the new education will have to come from institutions that are now training prospective teachers" (p. 136). The great obstacle, however, was that schools of education were themselves part of the overall problem because they, too, were mired in the old education. Postman and Weingartner say as much in a discussion of methods courses offered in teacher education programs across the country in the late 1960s. Speaking of "content" and "methods" courses, they at one point state:

> Everyone knows that the "real" courses are the content courses . . . The "fake" courses are the methods courses, those conspiracies of emptiness which are universally ridiculed because their finest ambition is to instruct in how to write lesson plans, when to use an overhead projector, and why it is desirable to keep the room at a comfortable temperature. (p. 19)

Having located a main source of the problem of the "old education" in schools of education, Postman and Weingartner believed that "if methods courses could be redesigned to be model learning environments, the educational revolution might begin" (p. 151). They also believed that any redesigning of methods courses must be founded on this understanding:

> *There can be no significant innovation in education that does not have at its center the attitudes of teachers, and it is an illusion to think otherwise.* The beliefs, feelings, and assumptions of teachers are the air of the learning environment; they determine the quality of life within it. (p. 33, italics in the original)

My focus on Postman and Weingartner's ideas will have to rest here (for now) because I have arrived at the most direct articulation between their ideas and mine.[1] Postman and Weingartner believed that the most powerful methods course was one that created situations in which preservice teachers could discover and examine their assumptions, beliefs, and knowledge about a range of educational issues. This is what I have attempted to do in the methods course that I have designed and teach, as I will explain later in this essay.

Before turning to that discussion of my methods course, though, I think it is important to explain another aspect of my teaching, one that is intricately bound up with my work in teacher education.

---

[1] Postman and Weingartner developed a general teaching methods course that they describe in some detail in their book, and for readers interested in their description of that course and the "inquiry theory" that informed it, I can only enact here that most cherished of gestures in every seventh-grader's performance of a book report: I recommend the book for you to take up on your own.

## A Critical Pedagogy of "Short Circuits"

In this section, I am imagining teacher educators whose situations are much like mine in that you teach methods courses or other courses to elementary, middle, or secondary preservice teachers, and you *also* teach a graduate course (maybe more) for masters and/or doctoral students, a course in which "high theory" is central.[2] For example, I teach a course called "Cultural Studies and Education" for doctoral and masters students in our Culture, Curriculum, and Change Ph.D. program.

An important aspect of the course is what I call a "pedagogy of 'short circuits.'" What do I mean by "short circuits"? This is a conceptualization derived from the Slovenian philosopher, Lacan-explicator, and Marxist Slavoj Zizek. Zizek (1992a) explains in the preface to his book *Looking Awry: An Introduction to Jacques Lacan through Popular Culture*, the subversive "reading" procedure he engages in to interpret Lacanian theory through popular culture:

> A reading of the most sublime theoretical motifs of Jacques Lacan together with and through exemplary cases of contemporary mass culture: not only Alfred Hitchcock . . . but also *film noir*, science fiction, detective novels, sentimental kitsch, and up—or down—to Stephen King. We thus apply to Lacan himself his own famous formula "Kant with Sade," i.e., his reading of Kantian ethics through the eyes of Sadian perversion. What the reader will find in this [Zizek's] book is a whole series of "Lacan with . . .": Alfred Hitchcock, Fritz Lang, Ruth Rendell, Patricia Highsmith, Colleen McCullough, Stephen King, etc. (If, now and then, the book also mentions "great" names like Shakespeare and Kafka, the reader need not be uneasy: they are read strictly as kitsch authors, on the same level as McCullough and King.) (p. viii)

Years later, in the Foreword to his book *The Parallax View*, Zizek (2006) explains what happens through engaging in this subversive, critical reading procedure:

> A short circuit occurs when there is a faulty connection in the network—faulty, of course, from the standpoint of the network's smooth functioning. Is not the shock of short-circuiting, therefore, one of the best metaphors for critical reading? Is not one of the most effective critical procedures to cross wires that do not usually touch: to take a major classic (text, author, notion), and read it in a short-circuiting way, through the lens of a 'minor' author, text, or conceptual apparatus . . . ? If the minor

---

[2] Of course, another imagined group is graduate students who are taking these "high theory" courses and who are also teaching and/or supervising student teachers. So in this section, I am actually imagining two groups who share the same challenge that I mention later in the discussion.

reference is well chosen, such a procedure can lead to insights which completely shatter and undermine our common perceptions. (p. ix)[3]

Zizek's "short circuiting" reading procedure not only brings about a unique method of teaching his readers Lacanian theory, but it also offers educators a pedagogical method for engaging students in theoretical explorations. In the rest of this section, I will discuss how, as part of the cultural studies graduate course, I engaged students in a series of critical readings that involved this procedure of short-circuiting and crossing the wires of major "social theory" texts by reading them with (alongside, through) minor texts, which were all popular films.

One main purpose of the course is to critique what Horkheimer and Adorno (2002) called "the culture industries" and the role that media play in what Guy Debord (2002) called (in the title of his classic work) *The Society of the Spectacle*. The students and I engage in our critique partly through Naomi Klein's (2002) brilliant book *No Logo*, which is an elegant analysis of the omnipresent corporate practice of branding. In reading *No Logo*, we create an interactive (or constructivist) cultural studies seminar by focusing in class on a variety of media texts—film, music, visual representations, Internet Web sites, YouTube videos, to name a few—that articulate with some aspect of *No Logo*. Put another way, we create a discursive "mosh pit," of sorts (see Trier, 2007).

Another main purpose of the course is to study in depth some of the core concepts and theories (from a Marxist tradition) that have been central to both cultural studies and educational discourses, including ideology, power, reification, hegemony, representation, subjectivity, the carnivalesque, strategies and tactics, habitus and cultural capital, and others. We read "classic" works of social theory by figures such as Lukacs, Gramsci, Althusser, Horkheimer and Adorno, Foucault, Debord, de Certeau, Bourdieu, and others, and the particular kind of cultural studies approach we take is that of "short circuits," which is to say that we view (or, in a cultural studies register, we "read") a film in tandem *with* a theoretical reading (readings and films are taken up as assigned texts outside of the class). For example, we read the theory and method of dialectics (Ollman, 2003) with *I ♥ Huckabees*; Lukacs's (1971) theorization of the concept of reification with the film *The Matrix*;

---

[3] Along with *Looking Awry*, other books in which Zizek engages in this procedure of reading major texts with and through minor texts include *Enjoy Your Symptom! Jacques Lacan in Hollywood and out* (Zizek, 2002) and *Everything You Always Wanted to Know about Lacan but Were Afraid to Ask Hitchcock* (edited by Zizek, 1992b).

Horkheimer and Adorno's (2002) critique of the culture industries with the film *Network*; Althusser's (1971) theorization of repressive and ideological state apparatuses with the documentary *The War at Home*; Gramsci's (1988) development of the concept of hegemony with the documentary *Manufacturing Consent*; Foucault's (1987a) theory of power with *The Paper Chase*; Bourdieu's (1984) concepts of habitus and cultural capital with *Educating Rita*; Bahktin's (1968) theorization of the carnivalesque (Stallybrass & White, 1986) with *Pump Up the Volume*; de Certeau's theorization of strategies and tactics and *Dazed and Confused*; and others. The purpose of articulating "classic" social theory texts with cinematic texts is to discover how the texts can synergistically bring out clarifications of and a multiplicity of meanings in one another.

What has all this got to do with my work in teacher education? *Everything!*

My reason for discussing the "Cultural Studies and Education" course is that I want to highlight what I think is a common experience for those of us who teach both in doctoral programs and in teacher education programs, which is that *as* we are engaged in our teaching about critical social theories in our doctoral (or non-teacher education) graduate courses, *we have all likely wrestled simultaneously with the complex challenge of how to translate those theoretical discourses into our work with preservice teachers*. For me, just as the pedagogy of "short circuits" has been invaluable in my doctoral course, it has been the same in my methods course. Also, many of the theories that I teach in the doctoral course are taken up in the methods course.[4]

## Theoretical Engagements

In this section, I offer brief descriptions of some of the "short circuits" critical projects I have designed to involve preservice teachers in what I'll call *theoretical engagements*. It is essential to point out that the distinguishing features of these projects are that each (1) introduces a particular social or analytical theory through one or more academic texts; (2) articulates that theory with one or more media texts, usually a school film[5]; (3) engages preservice teach-

---

[4] I am the English Education professor in our Master of Arts in Teaching (MAT) program. Ours is a one-year program in which students take courses during the summer and fall and also observe one day each week in their mentor teacher's classroom; students teach during the spring semester and finish with culminating courses the following summer. I teach a methods course during the fall semester.

[5] I define school films as films that are in some way, even incidentally, about an educator or a student. Some well-known school films are *Mr. Holland's Opus*, *Dead Poets Society*,

ers in critical analyses that draw upon both the theoretical and media texts; and (4) involves preservice teachers in applying their theoretical understandings to actual classrooms, either through designing curricula, critically reflecting on phenomena they observe during their practicum experience, and/or engaging in enactments of the critical pedagogy modeled during the English methods course.

In one project (Trier, 2001b), I drew upon academic readings and school films for a particular pedagogical aim that involved problematizing preservice teachers' "autonomous," traditional notions of literacy (Street, 1984) by having them read Gee's (1996) articulation of Discourses and multiple literacies, and then having them view the film *Teachers* for its construction of literacy.[6] Through close readings of both the academic and cinematic texts, students challenged the film's assumption that literacy is merely the ability to pass standardized tests, and they opened up to a more sophisticated conceptualization based on Gee's definition of literacy as being the mastery of a secondary discourse. A project similar to this one involved analyzing Truffaut's classic film *The 400 Blows* for the cinematic literacy narrative it constructs and for how power operates to disempower marginalized students through traditional literacy discourses (Trier, 2007).

In another project, I introduced the concepts of habitus and cultural capital by having preservice teachers take up selected readings by Bourdieu (1984), Apple (1990), and Fiske (1987), and then viewing films such as *Educating Rita*, *School Ties*, and *Disturbing Behavior*. Each of these films takes place in an educational setting and presents characters who struggle to become recognized members of a particular habitus that is different from their own. After analyzing the films, preservice teachers described—in terms of habitus and cultural capital—their own social-economic-educational-cultural histories, and they also explained why some of their own students were more (or less) successful in school in part because the values and practices of their habiti were (or were not) prized by those of the schools they attended (Trier, 2002).

---

and *Dangerous Minds*. Some lesser-known school films are *Welcome to the Dollhouse* and *Elephant*. Some obscure school films are *Zero for Conduct* and *Torment*.

[6] I have capitalized the term "Discourse" here because Gee does so in his work. Gee (1996) defines "Discourse" in this way: "A Discourse is a socially accepted association among ways of using language, other symbolic expressions, and 'artifacts,' of thinking, feeling, believing, valuing, and acting that can be used to identify oneself as a member of a socially meaningful group or 'social network,' or to signal (that one is playing) a socially meaningful 'role'" (p. 131). Though my use of the term "discourse" follows Gee in this article, I will not capitalize the term hereafter.

Another project engaged students in reexamining their views of power (Trier, 2003). I noticed that in seminar discussions and essays, when the term "power" arose, students tended to express a desire to (in one student's words) "get rid of power in the classroom," by which she meant that she would avoid being "authoritarian." I found this problematic for two reasons: one was that a teacher cannot "get rid of power in the classroom"—power is always at work (or in play); and another reason was the belief that power was always a negative force. To engage students in analyses of power, I introduced the idea of "techniques of power" by assigning students to read Gore's (1998) articulation of eight "techniques of power." Then, to further explore "techniques of power," we analyzed selected scenes from the film *The Paper Chase*. Each scene represented some aspect of the techniques of power (surveillance, normalization, exclusion, classification, distribution, individualization, totalization, and regulation). Students analyzed the film through the theoretical frame of techniques of power provided through the academic print readings, and what they wrote and discussed revealed that they had begun to acquire an understanding of how teaching inherently involved engaging in disciplinary practices of techniques of power, and how power can in certain situations be a positive force.

One final example I will give is of a project that I designed to discover preservice teachers' perceptions of "inner-city schools" (Trier, 2005), I assigned students to write an essay in which they were to explain what they expected to see in a typical inner-city school. I found that most of the responses were similar in their negativity, responses (quoted below) that lived up to the stereotypes about urban schools that are constructed by and circulate within the social, political, and media channels of discourse in our society: the school would be "run down"; teachers would be "burnt out"; the parents "wouldn't attend parent-teacher meetings"; and the students would be "violent," "using drugs, and getting in trouble with the law"; and so on. To explore why students held these assumptions, I had them next read McCarthy's (1998) article "Educating the American Popular: Suburban Resentment and the Representation of the Inner City in Contemporary Film and Television." McCarthy argues that many television programs and films have always created "the most poignantly sordid fantasies of inner-city degeneracy and moral decrepitude" (p. 32). After reading McCarthy's article, students analyzed how inner-city school films such as *The Principal*, *The Substitute*, and *187* construct "inner-city" students, teachers, schools, and the surrounding communities. Each of these films presents the very kind of "sordid fantasies" that McCarthy describes. Students next wrote essays comparing these cinematic constructions with their own previously articulated assumptions, beliefs, and knowledge about so-called inner-city schools. Most of the students realized their negative perceptions had derived from media, a realization that opened them to the possibility of unlearning their negative assumptions.

I consider the *theory-driven critical pedagogy* that I practice as a teacher educator, that I recommend to my students, and that I articulate in publications to be an important element in a process of preparing what can be described as the "new" teacher, one who would be central to bringing into existence what Postman and Weingartnen called the "new" education. Such a "new" teacher is someone who is theoretical and multidisciplinary, who holds a sociolinguistic perspective of literacy, who draws upon multiple texts (both academic print texts and media texts), and who thinks critically about how race, ethnicity, language, class, gender, power, and representation articulate with and shape a wide range of educational issues, practices, and structures.

## (Lost) in Translation

I ended the section "A Critical Pedagogy of 'Short Circuits'" by remarking on the *challenge* those of us who work with preservice teachers face in our efforts to translate critical social theories into what we teach in our teacher education courses. The assumption that I left unarticulated was *why* I think it is essential for us to engage preservice teachers theoretically in our courses. My most simply stated explanation for the value of theory is that new concepts provide us with the capacity to conceptualize phenomena in new, more sophisticated ways. New concepts can enable us to see what was not visible to us (intellectually) before. For me, it is not a matter of students acquiring a new set of terms and a new language merely to express "what they already know." If this were so, then theory would *not* be important because it would be little more than a discursive repackaging of familiar understandings. Rather, theory can alter—often radically—our familiar understandings by challenging our commonsense, everyday, taken-for-granted perceptions.

For example, through the theoretical engagements in the methods course, preservice teachers often engaged in their own *translation work* during their experiences in classrooms with their cooperating teachers. One main form that their translations took was in their *interpretations* of their experiences. As I have discussed in various articles, after I engage students in the theoretical projects, I then have students write critical essays during their fall semester observation practicum and also during their spring semester student teaching experience, essays in which they analyze what they are seeing. In the project concerning "power" (Trier, 2003), I found that my students explicitly adopted a discourse of power in their written reflections. By the end of the semester, they were engaged in seminar discussions of disciplinary power, of relations of power, and of techniques of power. They were deconstructing the power relationships embedded in the professional practices of their cooperating teachers, as when they problematized the use of marginalizing labels, and they also articulated critiques of systemwide practices, such as that of tracking. Most importantly, they explained how the discourse of power that they had begun to acquire would play an important role in shaping their own teaching practices, both during their student teaching and when they became full-time teachers. Without this new discourse of power, students would not (I argue) have engaged in these kinds of critical analyses because they would not have had the language to do so. (For more examples like this, see Trier 2001a, 2001b, 2002, 2003, 2005, 2006a, and 2007.)

At this point, one logical question (no doubt one of many) that the reader might pose is: What effects, if any, have the theoretical engagements and the pedagogy of "short circuits" modeled in the methods course had on the preservice teachers' own pedagogical practices? To answer this question, I need to expand my vision so that it includes a pedagogical scene that is the twin in importance to that of the methods course—that is, the mentor teacher's classroom. That is where a preservice teacher might be paired with a mentor teacher whose pedagogical orientation and practice resonate with what Postman and Weingartner called the "new education." On the other hand, the mentor teacher's classroom is also the site where a preservice teacher might end up being paired with a veteran teacher who is mired in the very same "old education" that Postman and Weingartner described.

My experience with mentor teachers has been quite mixed. Within my context, I compete with other nearby universities to find the best mentor teachers, and though I have been fortunate to have found many excellent mentors that I continue to pair up with preservice teachers every year, the real-world necessities of my context (not enough potential mentor teachers at the time when I need to make the placements, some great mentors retire or leave teaching, etc.) inevitably cause me every year to place many preservice teachers with practicing teachers whose names I have been given (by our Placement Office) but who I have not seen teach, and so I cannot tell if they will be good mentors. The result of this "mixed" situation plays out the same way every year. Some preservice teachers are paired with "new education" mentors, and so they have many opportunities to translate their theoretical engagements from the methods course into pedagogical practices during their student teaching. They engage in their own variations of a pedagogy of "short circuits" by, for example, drawing on popular culture texts in teaching canonical texts (for a discussion of this, see Trier, 2006b). And generally they discover that with excellent, open, welcoming, creative mentors, they have many opportunities to attempt to *sustain* what was begun in their methods courses by enacting a pedagogy that is theoretical and multidisciplinary, that emanates from a sociolinguistic perspective of literacy, that draws upon multiple texts, and that is critically informed by how race, ethnicity, language, class, gender, power, and representation articulate with and shape a wide range of educational issues, practices, and structures.

Conversely, and unfortunately, many of the preservice teachers in any given cohort end up with veteran teachers who (recalling here my earlier discussion of Postman and Weingartner) are mired in an "old education" world in which they perpetrate on a daily basis unimaginative, routine, teacher-centered practices that dull the senses of their students and teach them virtually nothing beyond learning how to be obedient subjects in stale, restrictive classrooms. Preservice teachers who are with such "old education" teachers are not able to engage in any variation of a pedagogy of "short circuits," typically because drawing on multiple texts—media texts and popular culture—is verboten. Print texts are privileged; the banking model of teaching that Freire (2000) famously critiqued predominates; the "mentor" teachers (for whom "subversion" is unthinkable) have long since acquiesced to the deskilling demands of end-of-year testing and the dictates of No Child Left Behind; and such teachers have lost all faith in their students, no longer really believing that they can learn; and they deploy a regime of discipline and punish without any qualms or pangs of pedagogical conscience.

And yet, bleak and barren as this situation sounds, even these teachers and their classrooms—arguably, *especially* these placements and classrooms—provide preservice teachers with rich possibilities, if not for enacting a "new education" pedagogy, then most definitely for theoretically critiquing the debilitating conditions of the classroom. In such classrooms, preservice teachers see on a daily basis how relations of power marginalize some students (typically those of color or those for whom English is not their first language) through various "techniques of power" (Foucault, 1987b; Gore, 1998), and privilege others (typically white, middle- and upper-middle class students); how "literacy" is assumed to be of the old, traditional type (Street, 1984) rather than of a sociolinguistic nature (Gee, 1996); how those students with cultural capital, derived from their high status habitus (Bourdieu, 1984), end up in the advanced prep courses while those from the working class end up in the low-tracked courses; and so on. Though the preservice teachers in these with such "mentor" teachers face many challenges in such classrooms, they are the preservice teachers who live out most deeply the experience of negotiating a terrain of their own within the Teacher Discourse structured not to sustain them during their student teaching but more to exploit them in the sense of controlling their work while all the while having them teach (which provides the "mentor" with a kind of spring vacation during the student teaching period).

That's the real world. For some preservice teachers, their mentors enable them to translate their theoretical engagements into pedagogical experimentations; for other preservice teachers, their "mentors" become obstacles that cause much to get "lost in translation."

## Back to the Future

In 1969, a rhetoric of "subversion" and "revolution" was in the air, so to speak, and Postman and Weingartner deployed such a rhetoric throughout their book (starting with the title).[7] What I find most interesting, however, is that for all their calls for societal revolution, the authors were very specific and detailed about the everyday actions that teachers can perform in practical ways on a small scale in their classrooms. In fact, Postman and Weingartner believed that radical, widespread changes in society begin with very simple actions of a local, situational nature. As they put it, "revolutions can be made" from even "small . . . shifts" in one's pedagogical activity (p. 38), and "a simple idea" can "change the entire direction of life in a society" (p. 98).

That's what Postman and Weingartner believed. How about you?

---

[7] Acknowledging that "[s]ubversion is a risky business" (p. 194), they nevertheless hoped for "the subversion of our existing educational system" (206). They believed that the impact of the new education that they described and called for would "be unique and revolutionary" (p. 27); that "schools must consciously remake themselves into training centers for 'subversion'" (p. 6); that the purpose of schools "is to subvert attitudes, beliefs, and assumptions that foster chaos and uselessness" (p. 15); that "a revolution in teacher training" (p. 142) was necessary because it will be "the teachers of the future" who "must bring this [educational] revolution off or it will not happen" (p. 141); that if education methods courses could be redesigned, "the educational revolution might begin" (p. 151); and more.

# RESPONSE

*Anne M. Phelan*

James Trier's essay is immensely helpful and hopeful. Short-circuit pedagogy, as the author describes it, is dedicated to promoting and sustaining teachers' thinking about the circulation of power and the mutual entanglements of our social and educational worlds. Asserting the desirability and possibility of such a pedagogy, the author provides vivid images of practices for a different kind of teacher education. Two qualities of James' practice impress.

First, implicit in the author's pedagogy is the cultivation of discernment. Discernment speaks to the capacity to see the significance of a text or event, to imagine various responses, and to judge ethically how one ought to respond (Phelan, 2005). Choosing a response means being able to discriminate the relevant details (Kessels & Korthagen, 1996). Learning to discriminate involves prioritizing the particulars given in the text or experience, constructing their significance in light of reading and conversations with oneself and others, and finally, making judgments about how to respond. In James' classroom, teacher candidates engage with the particulars of cultural artifacts (e.g., film) alongside the general propositions of theoretical texts (e.g., Bourdieu); in doing so, they engage in the very play of thought that characterizes the practice of teaching.

Second, the play of thought and the posing of value-rational questions about education (e.g., What is desirable? Who gains? Who loses?) (Flyvberg, 2001) recast the classroom, and the profession itself, as a public space for dialogue about human flourishing. Teacher candidates learn to conceive of teaching as a little less private (and personal) than it often appears to be. Rather than view teaching as an autonomous act of an individual with the freedom to teach in accordance with one's personal beliefs, teaching can be seen as a struggle among multiple and often contradictory commitments. As such, James' approach supports a growing awareness of conflicting commitments and responsibilities to the profession, self, and others. It promotes an increasing willingness to identify and wrestle with the challenges of teaching and learning and to wonder out loud about a collective professional future. It advances an understanding of (professional) freedom as requiring the presence of others in making our (professional) lives together and in understanding ourselves (Coulter, 2002).

And yet, despite these grand and hopeful gestures, I am increasingly uneasy with the burden that the author places on teacher candidates and on teaching itself. Is there a danger that "short-circuit" pedagogy, however intellectually and politically compelling, becomes little more than the provocation for deep resentment and the manipulation of a generalized anxiety in teacher candidates? Neither, of course, is some form of sombre withdrawal the answer . . .

# We invite the reader to consider the following questions:

1. How do educators prevent "short-circuit" pedagogy from becoming another form of social engineering that assumes, instrumentally, that (teacher) education is like a car engine (if we make the right modifications in teaching, it will convey us to our destination—the promised land of a critical, democratic society)?

2. What intellectual resources are necessary if teacher educators and teacher candidates are to begin to complicate the messages of critical pedagogy so that it takes into consideration the psychic life of power and resistance in learning?

3. Phelan uses the phrase "social justice" once in her essay, just before a quote by Pinar (2004) about "social engineering. In her quote from Pinar, no definition of social justice is provided, nor does Phelan herself offer one. And yet, most educators likely would state that working toward the end of bringing about social justice is central to their work. What is your definition of social justice? And do you believe that what you are doing in the name of social justice can be construed as "social engineering"?

4. In your work as an educator, do you find yourself simultaneously working within and yet also challenging and subverting discourses of instrumental reason? If so, what means have you used to subvert the prescribed ends you are expected to bring about as a result of discourses infused by instrumental reasoning?

# Afterword

## *Fiona J Benson and Caroline Riches*

> "Would you tell me, please, which way I ought to go from here?"
> "That depends a good deal on where you want to get to," said the Cat.
> "I don't much care where—" said Alice.
> "Then it doesn't matter which way you walk," said the Cat.
> "—so long as I get *somewhere* ," Alice added as an explanation.
> "Oh, you're sure to do that," said the Cat, "if you only walk long enough."
> (Lewis Carroll, 1989, p. 104)

Unlike Alice, we do care where we want to get to in teacher education. We believe our shared destination is an understanding of teacher education that is informed and responds to a necessary and multifaceted, yet confluent, call to excellence. However, it is our contention, as evidenced by this book, that we should be less concerned with the most direct route to our destination and more ready to acknowledge and enter into the varied and at times challenging landscape we travel. As Joe Kincheloe remarked:

> simply put teacher education is ensnared in a swamp of complications. Those of us concerned with the future of the teaching profession and its central role in promoting a healthy, democratic society have no choice but to make sense of these complexities. (2004, p. 11)

Faculties of Education struggle with a split personality of sorts, where on the one hand we engage in the theory and philosophy of education whilst on the other we invest time and energy into the preparation of teachers. To the uninitiated there is a clear connection between these two pursuits, but to those of us in the know, there is often a lack of communication that prevents fruitful collaboration and creates a sense of division between our mutual goals.

We believe our colleagues would agree that conversation is a fairly accessible tool. What we might also agree upon is that we engage in this act not nearly enough—and often, only with those with whom we might share a familiar discourse. Our very educational endeavours, as concerned with the human condition as they may be, act to further the divide that hobbles opportunity to move ahead with the power of shared commitment and expertise.

The conversations in this book, through their exploration of different perspectives, goals, expectations, barriers and responsibilities around teacher education, have bridged this divide in substantive ways. The invitation to the reader is to undertake a thoughtful engagement of these ideas, as well as others, and carry on the conversation in ways that extend into the less familiar. It is our hope that you, the reader, will leave this book as a more informed and intrepid traveller in the landscape of teacher education. Perhaps you might even be tempted to say to Alice and the Cat "accompany me on my journey, we have much to talk about."

Our common axis in any study pertaining to education is to create a world that is better informed, just and humane. We believe that Joe would have been encouraged with the way in which the essays in this book have directed us away from the most direct route to our destination and engaged us in the broader and richer complexities along the way.

# References

AFT (n.d.). AFT—A Union of Professionals. "Who we are." Retrieved November 2, 2008, from http://www.aft.org/about/index.htm.

Altbach, P. (2004). Globalization and the university: Myths and realities in an unequal world. *Tertiary Education and Management, 1*, 1–20.

Althusser, L. (1971). *Lenin and philosophy and other essays* (B. Brewster, Trans.). New York: Monthly Review Press. (Original work published 1969.)

Apple, M. (1990). *Ideology and curriculum*. New York: Routledge.

Arendt, H. (1998). *The Human Condition*. Chicago: University of Chicago Press. (Original work published in 1958.)

Arendt, H. (2006). *Between past and future: Eight exercises in political thought*. New York: Penguin. (Original work published in 1961.)

Bakhtin, M. (1968). *Rabelais and his world*. Cambridge: Massachusetts Institute of Technology Press.

Ball, S. (2003). The teacher's soul and the terrors of performativity. *The Journal of Education Policy, 18* (2), 215–228.

Beck, C., & Kosnik, C. (2000). Associate teachers in pre-service education: Clarifying and enhancing their role. *Journal of Education for Teaching, 26*(3), 207–224.

Beck, C., & Kosnik, C. (2002a). Components of a good practicum placement: Student teacher perceptions. *Teacher Education Quarterly, 29* (2), 81–98.

Beck, C., & Kosnik, C. (2002b). Professors and the practicum: Involvement of university faculty in preservice practicum supervision. *Journal of Teacher Education. 29*(1), 6–19.

Beck, C., Freese, A., & Kosnik, C. (2004). Learning through self-study in a professional setting: The preservice practicum. In J. Loughran, M.L. Hamilton, V. LaBoskey, & T. Russel (Eds.) *International handbook of self-study of teaching and teacher education practices* (pp. 1259–1293). Dordecht, the Netherlands: Kluwer.

Benson, F. & Riches, C. (2008). Courses and practicum do not an honest program make: Mitigating the lament of betrayal in teacher education. *Canadian Association for Teacher Education Annual Conference*, Vancouver, BC.

Berliner, D. C., & Biddle, B. J. (1995). *The manufactured crisis*. New York: Addison-Wesley.

Bernstein, R. (2007). *Reflection submitted to the Maxine Greene Foundation for Social Imagination, the Arts and Education*. Retrieved October 2007 from http://www.Maxinegreene.org/ BOARD OF EDUCATION v. ROWLEY (1982) accessed at http://www.listen-up.org/dnload4/ rowley.pdf.

Board of Educ. v. Rowley, 458 U.S. 176 (1982).

Booth, T., & Ainscow, M. (1998) *From them to us: An international study of inclusion in education*. London: Routledge.

Borges, C., & Desbiens, J.-F. (2003). Conclusion. In C. Borges & J.-F. Desbiens (Eds.), *Savoir, former et intervenir dans une éducation physique en changement* (pp. 223–242). Sherbrooke, Québec, Canada: Éditions du CRP.

Boudreau, P., & Baria, A. (1998). La définition donnée par des enseignants associés de la supervision d'un stagiaire. In D. Raymond & Y. Lenoir (Eds.), *Enseignants de métier et formation initiale* (pp. 141–154). Brussels, Belgium: DeBoeck.

Bourdieu, P. (1984). *Distinction: A social critique of the judgment of taste*. Cambridge, MA: Harvard University Press.

Braslavsky, C. (2001). Increasing demand but inadequate conditions: A keynote address at the 46th World Assembly of the International Council of Education for Teaching, Santiago, Chile, July 2001.

Brawdy, P., & Byra, M. (1995). Supervision of preservice teachers during an early field teaching experience. *Physical Educator, 52* (3), 1–13.

Brennan, M., & Zipin, L. (2008). Neo-colonization of cultural struggles for justice in Australian education and teacher education. In A. Phelan & J. Sumsion (Eds.), *Critical readings in teacher education: Provoking absences* (pp. 99–114). Rotterdam, The Netherlands: Sense Publishers.

British Columbia College of Teachers (1998). Results of 1997 survey of graduates of BC teacher education programs. Retrieved from http://www.bcct.ca/forms.aspx#5.

British Columbia College of Teachers (2001). Results of 2000 survey of graduates of BC teacher education programs. Retrieved from http://www.bcct.ca/forms.aspx#5.

British Columbia College of Teachers (2004). Results of 2003 survey of graduates of BC teacher education programs. Retrieved from http://www.bcct.ca/forms.aspx#5.

British Columbia Ministry of Education (2008). Curriculum for social responsibility performance standards. Retrieved from http://www.bced.gov.bc.ca/perf_stands/social_resp.htm.

# References

Britzman, D. (1991). *Practice makes practice: A critical study of learning to teach.* Albany: State University of New York Press.
Britzman, D. (1998). *Lost subjects, contested objects: Toward a psychoanalytic inquiry of learning.* Albany: State University of New York Press.
Britzman, D. (2003). *Practice makes practice: A critical study of learning to teach.* (Rev. ed.). Albany: State University of New York Press.
Brunelle, J., & Brunelle, J.-P. (1999). *Un système de supervision de la maîtrise des compétences de base dans l'enseignement de l'éducation physique et à la santé.* Unpublished manuscript.
Brunelle, J., Drouin, D., Godbout, P., & Tousignant, M. (1988). *La supervision de l'intervention en activité physique.* Montréal, Québec, Canada: Gaëtan Morin.
Bruner, J. (1985). Narrative and paradigmatic modes of thought. In Elliot W. Eisner (Ed.), *Learning and teaching the ways of knowing* (pp. 97–115). Chicago: University of Chicago Press.
Buckingham, D. (2003). *Media education: Literacy, learning and contemporary culture.* London: Polity.
Buckingham, D., & Sefton-Green, J. (1994). *Cultural studies goes to school.* New York: Routledge.
Building Classroom Relationships [Special section]. (2003). *Educational Leadership, 61* (1), 6–70.
Bujold, N. (2002). La supervision pédagogique. Vue d'ensemble. In M. Boutet & N. Rousseau (Eds.), *Les enjeux de la supervision pédagogique des stages* (pp. 9–23). Sainte-Foy, Québec, Canada: Les Presses de l'Université Laval.
Bullough, R. V., & Gitlin, A. D. (1995). *Becoming a student of teaching: methodologies for exploring self and school context.* New York Garland.
Burbules, N. C., & Warnick, B. R. (2006). Philosophical inquiry. In J. L. Green, G. Camilli, & P. B. Elmore (Eds.), *Handbook of complementary methods in education research* (pp. 489–502). Mahwah, NJ: Erlbaum.
Bush, G. W. (2004), The essential work of democracy. *Phi Delta Kappan, 86* (2), p. 114, 118–121.
Butler, J. (2002). What is critique? An essay on Foucault's virtue. In D. Ingram (Ed.), *The political: Readings in continental philosophy* (pp. 212–226). London: Basil Blackwell.
Calderhead, J. (1987). *Exploring teachers' thinking.* London: Cassell.
Calderhead, J., & Shorrock, S. B. (1997). *Understanding teacher education: case studies in the professional development of beginning teachers.* London: Falmer Press.

Cameron, S. (1995). *On the take: Crime, corruption, and greed in the Mulroney years.* Toronto, Ontario, Canada: McClelland-Bantam.

Carlier, G. (2002). Superviser des stagiaires en éducation physique: balises pour une fonction en voie de professionnalisation. *Avante, 8* (1), 96–111.

Carroll, L. (1989). *Alice's adventures in wonderland.* New York: Bantam Books.

Carter, K., & Doyle, W. (1996). Personal narrative and life history in learning to teach. In J. Sikula, T. J. Buttery, & E. Guyton (Eds.), *Handbook of research on teacher education: A project of the Association of Teacher Educators* (2nd ed., pp. 120–142). New York: Simon & Schuster Macmillan.

Casey, M., & Howson, P. (1993). Educating preservice students based on a problem-centered approach to teaching. *Journal of Teacher Education, 44*(5), 361-369.

Castoriadis, C. (2007). *Figures of the thinkable.* Stanford, CA: Stanford University Press.

Chaliès, S., & Durand, M. (2000). L'utilité discutée du tutorat en formation initiale des enseignants. *Recherche et Formation, 35,* 145–180.

Charles, H. (1999). *UNESCO Maputo position on HIV/AIDS prevention education.* Unpublished manuscript.

Clifford, G., & Guthrie, J. (1988). *Ed school: A brief for professional education.* Chicago: University of Chicago Press.

Cochran-Smith, M. (1998). Teaching for social change: Toward a grounded theory of teacher education. In. A. Hargreaves, A. Lieberman, M. Gullajn, & D. Hopkins (Eds.), *The International Handbook of Educational Change.* Dordrecht, The Netherlands: Kluwer.

Cochran-Smith, M. (2004). *Walking in the road. Race, diversity and social justice in teacher education.* New York: Teachers College Press.

Cochran-Smith, M., & Fries, S. (2006). Researching teacher education in changing times: Politics and paradigms. In M. Cochran-Smith & K. Zeichner (Eds.), *Studying teacher education: The report of the AERA Panel on Research and Teacher Education* (pp. 69–109). Mahwah, NJ: Lawrence Erlbaum.

Cochran-Smith, M., & Zeichner, K. M. (Eds.) (2005). *Studying teacher education: The report of the AERA Panel on Research and Teacher Education.* Mahwah, NJ: Lawrence Erlbaum.

Cohen, A. (2006). *Attending to the inner life of an educator: The human dimension in education.* Unpublished doctoral dissertation, University of British Columbia, Vancouver, Canada. Retrieved April 1, 2007, from https://dspace.library.ubc.ca/dspace/handle/2429/63.

Cole, A. (1999). Teacher educators and teacher education reform: Individual commitments, institutional realities. *Canadian Journal of Education, 24* (3), 281–295.

Cole, A. (2000a). Case studies of reform in Canadian preservice teacher education. *Alberta Journal of Educational Research, 46* (2), 192–195.

Cole, A. (2000b). Toward a preliminary understanding of teacher education reform in Anglophone Canada. *McGill Journal of Education, 35* (2), 139–154.

Cole, A., Knowles, G., & Luciano, T. (Eds.) (2004). *Provoked by art: Theorizing arts-informed research.* Halifax, Nova Scotia, Canada: Backalong Books.

Comité d'orientation de la formation du personnel enseignant (COFPE) (2005). *La formation en milieu de pratique. De nouveaux horizons à explorer.* Québec, Canada: Gouvernement du Québec.

Commonwealth Secretariat & Maritime Centre of Excellence for Women's Health. (2002). *Gender Mainstreaming in HIV/AIDS: Taking a Multisectoral Approach.* London, UK: Commonwealth Secretariat.

Considine, M. (2006). Theorizing the university as a cultural system: Distinctions, identities, emergencies. *Educational Theory, 56* (3), 255–270.

Coulter, D. (2002). What counts as action in educational action research? *Educational Action Research 10* (2): 189–206.

Coulter, D. (2006). *Beginning without an end in mind: Educational power.* Unpublished manuscript.

Coulter, D., Daniel, M., Decker, E., Essex, P., Naslund, J., et al. (2007). A question of judgment: A response to Standards for the Education, Competence and Professional Conduct of Educators in British Columbia. *Educational Insights, 11* (3). Retrieved from www.ccfi.educ.ubc.ca/publication/insights/v11no3/articles/coulter.html.

Cowley, P., & Easton, S. T. (2003). *The $100,000,000 giveaway: Who says education doesn't get enough money?* Vancouver, BC, Canada: The Fraser Institute.

Creating Caring Schools [Special section]. (2003). *Educational Leadership, 60* (6), 6–78.

Crocker, R., Dibbon, D., & Glickman, V. (2007). Proposed study of teacher preparation programs across Canada. Kelowna, BC: Society for the Advancement of Excellence in Education. Retrieved from http://www.saee.ca/research/B_019_DDD_MID.php.

Dale, R. (1999). Specifying globalization effects on national policy: A focus on the mechanisms. *Journal of Education Policy, 14* (1), 1–17.

Dale, R. (2001). Constructing a long spoon for comparative education: Charting the career of the "New Zealand model." *Comparative Education, 37* (4), 493–500.

Dale, R. (2005). Globalisation, knowledge economy and comparative education. *Comparative Education, 41* (2), 117–149.

Damasio, A. (1999). *The feeling of what happens: Body and emotion in the making of consciousness.* San Diego, CA: Harcourt.

Dare, M. (2002). *How can teachers' qualifications be upgraded?* Retrieved from Society for Quality Education Web site: http://www.societyforquality education.org/teachers/9.html.

Dare, M., Hepburn, C. R., & Merrifield, J. (2006). *Why Canadian education isn't improving.* Vancouver, BC, Canada: The Fraser Institute.

Darling-Hammond, L. (1998). Teachers and teaching: Testing policy hypotheses from a national commission report. *Educational Researcher, 27* (1), 5–15.

Darling-Hammond, L. (2000a). How teacher education matters. *Journal of Teacher Education, 51* (3), 166–173.

Darling-Hammond, L. (2000b). Reforming teacher preparation and licensing: Debating the evidence. *Teachers College Record, 102* (1), 28–56.

Darling-Hammond, L. (2000c). Teacher quality and student achievement: A review of the state policy evidence. *Education Policy Analysis Archives, 8* (1). Retrieved April 20, 2007, from http://epaa.asu.edu/epaa/v8n1/.

Darling-Hammond, L. (Ed.) (2005). *Professional development schools: Schools for developing a profession.* New York: Teachers College Press.

Darling-Hammond, L. (2006). Constructing 21st-century teacher education. *Journal of Teacher Education, 57* (3), 300–314.

Darling-Hammond, L., & Baratz-Snowden, J. (2005). *A good teacher in every classroom: Preparing the highly qualified teachers our children deserve.* San Francisco: Jossey-Bass.

Darling-Hammond, L., & Bransford, J. (Eds.) (2005). *Preparing teachers for a changing world: What teachers should learn and be able to do.* San Francisco: Jossey-Bass.

Darling-Hammond, L., Hammerness, K., Grossman, P., Rust, F., & Shulman, L. (2005). The design of teacher education programs. In L. Darling-Hammond & J. Bransford (Eds.), *Preparing teachers for a changing world: What teachers should learn and be able to do* (pp. 390–441). San Francisco: Jossey-Bass.

Davies, B., & Bansel, P. (2007). Neoliberalism and education. *International Journal of Qualitative Studies in Education, 20* (3), 247–259.

de Certeau, M. (1984). *The practice of everyday life.* Berkeley: University of California Press.

De Lange, N., Mitchell, C., & Stuart, J. (Eds.) (in press). *Putting people in the picture.* Amsterdam: Sense.

Debord, G. (2002). *The society of the spectacle.* New York: Zone Books. (Original work published 1967.)

Deiro, J. A. (1996). *Teaching with heart: Making healthy connections with students.* Thousand Oaks, CA: Corwin Press.

Derrida, J. (1992). *The other heading: Reflections on today's Europe* (P. A. Brault & M. B. Naas, Trans.). Bloomington: Indiana University Press. (Original work published 1991.)

Derrida, J. (2001). *On cosmopolitanism and forgiveness* (M. Dooley & M. Hughes, Trans.). London: Routledge. (Original work published 1997.)

Desbiens, J.-F., Brunelle, J.-P., Spallanzani, C., & Roy, M. (2006). Mejorar el acompañamiento de los pasantes en enseñanza en educación física a través de la formación para la supervisión de los profesores asociados. Un proyecto en vías de elaboración en la Facultad de Educación Física y Deportiva (FEFD) de la Universidad de Sherbrooke. *Revista de Educación*, 339 (janvier-avril), 339–361. Retrieved from: http://www.revistaeducacion.mec.es/re339_14.htm

Desbiens, J.-F., Spallanzani, C., Brunelle, J.-P., Turcotte S., & Roy, S. (2006). *Concevoir autrement la formation à l'accompagnement des stagiaires en enseignement de l'éducation physique et sportive (ÉPS) pour faire évoluer les pratiques de supervision.* XXIII<sup>e</sup> Congrès de l'AIPU, 15 au 18 mai 2006, Monastir, Tunisie.

Dewey, J. (1974). The relation of theory to practice in education. In R. Archambault (Ed.), *John Dewey on education: Selected writings* (pp. 313–339). Chicago: University of Chicago Press. (Original work published 1904.)

Dewey, J. (1975). *Moral principles in education.* Carbondale, IL: Southern Illinois University Press. (Original work published 1909.)

Dougherty, S. (2006, August 12). Teachers need training. *The [Montreal] Gazette*, p. L8.

Doyle, W., & Carter, K. (2003). Narrative and learning to teach: Implications for teacher-education curriculum. *Journal of Curriculum Studies 35* (2), 129–137.

Dyson, L. L., & Zhang, N. (2004). Concerns about the integration of elementary school children with disabilities: A comparison of Canadian and Chinese teachers. *Exceptionality Education Canada, 14* (2&3), 141–167.

Education deans still working on improvements to teaching and teachers. (2007, May 28). *University of Melbourne News*. Retrieved from http://uninews.unimelb.edu .au/view.php?articleID=4252.

Elmore, R. F., & McLaughlin, M. W. (1988). *Steady work*. Washington, DC: National Institute for Education.

Ethell, R. G., & McMeniman, M. (2000). Unlocking the knowledge in action of expert practitioners. *Journal of Teacher Education, 51* (2), 87–101.

Evertson, C., Hawley, W., & Zlotnik, M. (1985). Making a difference in educational quality through teacher education. *Journal of Teacher Education, 36* (3), 2–10.

Falkenberg, T. (2006). *Caring and human agency: Foundations of an approach to teacher education*. Unpublished doctoral dissertation, Simon Fraser University, Burnaby, British Columbia, Canada. Retrieved from http://hdl.handle.net/1892/3769.

Falkenberg, T. (in press). On the grounding of teacher education in the human condition. *Journal of Educational Thought*.

Feiman-Nemser, S. (1983). Learning to teach. In L. Shulman & G. Sykes (Eds.), *Handbook of teaching and policy* (pp. 150–170). New York: Longman.

Fenstermacher, G. D. (1990). Some moral considerations on teaching as a profession. In J. I. Goodlad, R. Soder, & K. A. Sirotnik (Eds.), *The moral dimensions of teaching* (pp. 130–151). San Francisco: Jossey-Bass.

Finley, S. (2000) Transformative teaching for multicultural classrooms: Designing curriculum and classroom strategies for master's level teacher education. *Multicultural Education, 7* (3), 20–27.

Finn, C., & Kanstoroom, K. (2000). *Improving, empowering, dismantling*. Washington, DC: Thomas B. Fordham Foundation.

Fiske, J. (1987). *Television culture*. London: Methuen.

Fitzsimmons, P. (2000). Changing conceptions of globalization: Changing conceptions of education. *Educational Theory, 50* (4), 505–520.

Flyvberg, B. (2001). *Making Social Science Matter*. London: Cambridge University Press.

Ford, N., Oddalo, D., & Chorlton, R. (2003). Communication from a human rights perspective: Responding to the HIV/AIDS pandemic in Eastern and Southern Africa. *Journal of Health Communication, 8*, 519–612.

Foucault, M. (1987a). Docile bodies. In P. Rabinow (Ed.), *The Foucault Reader*. New York: Pantheon Books.

Foucault, M. (1987b). The body of the condemned. In P. Rabinow (Ed.), *The Foucault Reader*. New York: Pantheon Books.

Foucault, M. (1987c). The means of correct training. In P. Rabinow (Ed.), *The Foucault Reader*. New York: Pantheon Books.

Frappier, J.-Y., & Canadian Association for Adolescent Health. (2006). Sexual Knowledge, Attitudes and Behaviours of Canadian Teenagers and Mothers of Teens. *ProTeen, 15*(1-2), 3-18.

Freire, P. (2000). *Pedagogy of the oppressed*. New York: Continuum. (Original work published 1970.)

Freire, P. (1998). *Teachers as cultural workers: Letters to those who dare to teach*. Boulder, CO: Westview Press.

Furlong, J., Barton, L., Miles, S., Whiting, C., & Whitty, G. (2000). *Teacher education in transition: Re-forming professionalism?* Buckingham, England: Open University Press.

Gadamer, H.-G. (1989). *Truth and method* (2nd, rev. ed.). New York: Continuum. (Original work published 1960.)

Gauthier, C., Desbiens, J., Malo, A., Martineau, S., & Simard, D. (1997). *Pour une pédagogie de la pratique: recherches contemporaines sur le savoir des enseignants*. Québec: Presses de l'Université Laval.

Gee, J. (1996). *Social linguistics and literacies: Ideology in discourses*. Bristol, PA: Falmer Press.

Gervais, C. (1997). Spécificité du rôle du superviseur universitaire. In M. Tardif & H. Ziarko (Eds.), *Continuités et ruptures dans la formation des maîtres au Québec*. Sainte-Foy, Québec, Canada: Presses de l'Université Laval.

Gilford, S., (2008, August 5). NEA spends millions for political influence. *Wall Street Journal*. Retrieved 16/November/2008/ from http://online.wsj.com/article/SB121789217510411697.html.

Giroux, H. (2002). Neoliberalism, corporate culture, and the promise of higher education: The university as a democratic public sphere. *Harvard Educational Review, 72* (4), 1–37.

Glassford, L. (1997, June). Meeting the needs of future teachers: Curricular changes for preservice programs from implications of secondary teachers' perceptions of recent changes in Ontario schools. Paper presented at the annual meeting of the Canadian Association for Teacher Education, St. John's, Newfoundland.

Glickman, C., & Bey, T. (1990). Supervision. In W. R. Houston (Ed.), *Handbook of research on teacher education* (pp. 549–566). New York: Macmillan.

Goldstein, L. S. (2002). *Reclaiming caring in teaching and teacher education*. New York: Peter Lang.

Gómez, A., & Meacham, D. (1998). Women & HIV/AIDS: A gender perspective. In A. Gómez & D. Meacham (Eds.), *Women, Vulnerability and HIV/AIDS: A Human Rights Perspective*. Santiago, Chile: Latin American and Caribbean Women's Health Network.

Goodlad, J. I. (1990). *Teachers for our nation's schools*. San Francisco: Jossey-Bass.

Gootman, M. E. (2000). *The caring teacher's guide to discipline: Helping young students learn self-control, responsibility, and respect* (2nd ed.). Thousand Oaks, CA: Corwin Press.

Gore, J. (1998). Disciplining bodies: On the continuity of power relations in pedagogy. In T. Popkewitz & M. Brennan (Eds.), *Foucault's challenge: Discourse, knowledge, and power in education*. New York: Routledge.

Gould, H. (2007, February 7). What's culture got to do with HIV/AIDS? *Findings, Health World Links*. Retrieved from www.healthlinks.org.uk.

Gould, H., & Marsh, M. (2004). *Culture: Hidden development*. London: Creative Exchange.

Gramsci, A. (1988). *The Gramsci reader: Selected writings, 1916–1935*. New York: New York University Press.

Greene, M. (1998). Introduction: Teaching for social justice. In W. Ayers, J. A. Hunt, & T. Quinn (Eds.), *Teaching for social justice* (pp. xxvii–xlvi). New York: Teachers College Press.

Griffiths, M., et al. (2003). *Action for social justice in education*. Maidenhead, England: Open University Press.

Grimmett, P. P. (1992). Trends and issues in teacher education in English speaking Canada. *The Teacher Educator 27* (4), 12–20.

Grimmett, P. P. (1995). Crafting the curriculum of teacher education. In S. Majhanovich, (Ed.). *Re-forming teacher education: Problems and prospects* (pp. 55–76). London, Ontario, Canada: Althouse Press.

Grimmett, P. P. (1998). Reconceptualizing the practice of teacher education: On not throwing out the concurrent model with the reform bathwater. *The Alberta Journal of Educational Research, 44* (3), 251–267.

Grimmett, P. P. (2008, March). Accreditation in an era of professional governance: Protecting the public interest or bureaucratic expansionism? Paper presented at the annual meeting of the American Educational Research Association, New York, NY.

Grimmett, P. P., & Echols, F. H. (2006). *What say we dance but this time with music: Review of the provisions of Regulation 347/02, Accreditation of Teacher Education Programs in Ontario*. Toronto, Canada: Ontario College of Teachers.

Grossman, P. L. (1990). *The making of a teacher: Teacher knowledge and teacher education.* New York: Teachers College Press.

Haberman, M. (1985). Does teacher education make a difference? A review of comparisons between liberal arts and teacher education graduates. *Journal of Thought, 20* (2), 25–34.

Hadot, P. (1995). *Philosophy as a way of life: Spiritual exercises from Socrates to Foucault* (M. Chase, Trans.). Oxford: Blackwell. (Original work published 1987.)

Hagger, H., & McIntyre, D. (2006). *Learning teaching from teachers: Realizing the potential of school-based teacher education.* Maidenhead, England: Open University Press.

Ham, V., & Kane, R. G., (2004). Finding a way through the swamp: A case for self-study as research. In J. Loughran, T. Russell, V. LaBoskey, & M. L. Hamilton (Eds.), *International handbook on self-study in teaching and teacher education* (pp. 103–150). Amsterdam: Kluwer Press.

Hamilton, M. L (Ed.). (1998). *Reconceptualizing teaching practice: Self-study in teacher education* (pp. 7–18). London: Falmer Press.

Hastings, W. (2004). Emotions and the practicum: The cooperating teachers' perspective. *Teachers and Teaching: Theory and Practice, 10* (2), 135–148.

Hawkins, V. J. (2007). Narrowing gaps for special-needs students. *Educational Leadership, 64* (5), 61–63.

Health Canada. (1999). Canadian Strategy on HIV/AIDS: Youth. Ottawa: Health Canada.

Health Canada (2003). HIV/AIDS Among Aboriginal Persons in Canada: A Continuing Concern. Epi Update. Retrieved from: http://www.hc-sc.gc.ca/pphb-dgspsp/publicat/epiu-aepi/hiv-vih/aborig_e.html, September 9, 2003.

Heidegger, M. (1962). *Being and time* (J. Macquarrie & E. Robinson, Trans.). New York: Harper & Row. (Original work published 1927.)

Henkel, M. (2007). Can academic autonomy survive in the knowledge society? A perspective from Britain. *Higher Education Research and Development, 26* (1), 87–99.

Hoban, G. (Ed.) (2005). *The missing links in teacher education design: Developing a multi-linked conceptual framework.* Amsterdam: Springer.

Horkheimer, M., & Adorno, M. (2002). The culture industry: Enlightenment as mass deception. In G. S. Noerr (Ed.) & E. Jephcott (Trans.), *Dialectic of enlightenment: Philosophical fragments.* Stanford, CA: Stanford University Press. (Original work published 1947.)

Horton, M. & Freire, P. (1990). *We make the road by walking: Conversations on education and social change.* B. Bell, J. Gaventa, J. Peters (Eds.) Philadelphia: Temple University Press.

Humes, W. M. (1994). Teacher education in British Columbia and Scotland: A response. *Journal of Education for Teaching, 20* (1), 47–57.

Hutchinson, N. (2004). Critical reflection by teacher candidates on cases based in their experience: Teacher education for inclusive education. *Exceptionality Education Canada, 14* (2&3), 89–114.

IDEIA (2004). The individuals with disabilities education improvement act of 2004. Retrieved November 11, 2008, from http://www.in.gov/ipas/2397.htm.

IES (2003). Education across levels: Funding for education, expenditure for education: 2003. Retrieved October 26, 2008, from http://nces.ed.gov/suveys/international/Intlindicators/index.asp?SectionNumber=1&SubSectionNumber=3&IndicatorNumber=101.

IES (n.d.). U.S. Dept of Education Institute of Education Sciences, National Center for Education Statistics. Retrieved October 26, 2008, from http://nces.ed.gov/fastfacts/.

ISBE (2006). 2006 Annual School Report. Illinois State Board of Education, Chicago, IL: Author.

ISBE (2008). 2008 School Report. Illinois State Board of Education, Chicago, IL: Author.

Johnson, D. (2005). *Signposts of success: Interpreting Ontario's elementary school test scores.* Toronto, Ontario, Canada: C. D. Howe Institute.

Johnson, D. (2007). *Ontario's best public schools: An update to* Signposts of success (2005). Toronto, Ontario, Canada: C. D. Howe Institute.

Jordan, A., & Stanovich, P. (2004). The beliefs and practices of Canadian teachers about including students with special education needs in their regular elementary classrooms. *Exceptionality Education Canada, 14* (2 & 3), 25–46.

Jordan, P., Phillips, M., & Brown, E. (2004). We train teachers: Why not supervisors and mentors? *Physical Educator, 61*(4), 219-221.

Kabeer, N. (2000). Social exclusion, poverty and discrimination: Towards an analytical framework. *IDS Bulletin, 31* (4), 83–97.

Kane, R. G. (2007). From naive practitioner to teacher educator and researcher: Constructing a personal pedagogy of teacher education. In T. Russell & J. Loughran (Eds.), *Enacting pedagogy of teacher education: Values, relationships and practices* (pp. 60–76). London: Routledge.

Kant, I. (1988). *Fundamental principles of the metaphysics of morals* (T. K. Abbott, Trans.). Amherst, NY: Prometheus Books. (Original work published 1785.)

Kennedy, M. (2006). Knowledge and vision in teaching. *Journal of Teacher Education 57* (3), 205–211.

Kessels, J., & Korthagen, F. (1996). The relationship between theory and practice: Back to the classics. *Educational Researcher,* 25 (3), 17–22.

Kincheloe, J. L. (2004). The bizarre, complex, and misunderstood world of teacher education. In J. L. Kincheloe, A. Bursztyn, & S. R. Steinberg (Eds.), *Teaching teachers: Building a quality school of urban education* (pp. 1–49). New York: Peter Lang.

King, R. (2007). Governance and accountability in the higher education regulatory state. *Higher Education, 53*, 411–430.

Klein, N. (2002). *No logo: No space, no choice, no jobs.* New York: Picador.

Knowles, G., & Cole, A. (2007). *Handbook of the arts in qualitative research: Perspectives, methodologies, examples and issues.* London: Sage.

Kohlberg, L. (with DeVries, R. et al.). (1987). *Child psychology and childhood education: A cognitive-developmental view.* New York: Longman.

Kohn, J. (2006). Introduction. In H. Arendt, *Between past and future: Eight exercises in political thought* (pp. vii–xxii). New York: Penguin.

Korthagen, F. (2001). *Linking practice and theory: The pedagogy of realistic teacher education.* London: Lawrence Erlbaum.

Kosnik, C. (1998). Conflicting and competing agendas: A school-university partnership for teacher education. In A. Cole, R. Elijah, & J. G. Knowles. (Eds.), *The heart of the matter: Teacher educators and teacher education reform* (pp. 193–210). San Francisco: Caddo Gap Press.

Kosnik, C., & Beck, C. (2003). The internship component of a teacher education program: Opportunities for learning. *The Teacher Educator, 39* (1) 18–34.

Kosnik, C., & Beck, C. (2007, April). What should be the main emphases in a preservice program? First and second year teachers' views. Paper presented at the American Educational Research Association annual conference, Chicago, IL.

Koster, B., Korthagen, F. A. J., & Wubbels, T. (1998). *European Journal of Teacher Education,* 21(1), 75–89.

Kozol, J. (2005), *The shame of the nation.* New York: Three Rivers.

Lacroix-Roy, F., Lessard, M., & Garant, C. (2003). *Étude sur les programmes de formation à l'accompagnement des stagiaires.* Québec, Canada: Table MEQ-Universités.

Lankshear, C., & Knobel, M. (2003). *New literacies*. London: Open University Press.

Lather, P. (1997). Troubling clarity: The politics of accessible language. *Harvard Educational Review, 66*, 525–545.

Lather, P. (2004). Applied Derrida: (Mis)reading the work of mourning in educational research. In P. P. Trifonas & M. A. Peters (Eds.), *Derrida, deconstruction and education: Ethics of pedagogy and research* (pp. 3–16). Oxford, England: Blackwell Publishing.

Lenski, S. D., Crawford, K., Crumpler, T., & Stallworth, C. (2005). Preparing preservice teachers in a diverse world. *Action in Teacher Education, 27* (3), 3–12.

Levine, R., McLaughlin, D., & Sietsema, J. (1996). *Trends in School District Demographics, 1986–87 to 1990–99* (Report No. NCES 96-399). Retrieved November 1, 2008, from http://nces.ed.gov/pubs96/96399.pdf.

Levinson, N. (2001). The paradox of natality. In M. Gordon (Ed.), *Hannah Arendt and education: Renewing our common world* (pp. 11–36). Boulder, CO: Westview Press.

Lewis, S. (2004). A pandemic within a pandemic. Statement by Stephen Lewis, UN Special Envoy for HIV/AIDS In Africa. XV International AIDS Conference, Bangkok, Sunday, July 11, 2004. Retrieved: http://www.wghi.org/Stephen_Lewis_Bangkok.pdf 26 August 2004.

Lewis, S. (2005). *Race against time*. Toronto: House of Anans Press.

Little, J. W. (1982). Norms of collegiality and experimentation: Workplace conditions of school success. *American Educational Research Journal, 19* (3), 325–340.

Loughran, J. (2006). *Developing a pedagogy of teacher education: Understanding teaching and learning about teaching*. London: Routledge.

Loughran, J. J., Hamilton, M. L., LaBoskey, V. K., & Russell, T. (Eds.) (2004). *International handbook of self-study of teaching and teacher education practice* (Vols. 1–2). Dordrecht, the Netherlands: Kluwer.

Lovelie, L. (2007). Education for deliberative democracy. In I. Gur Ze'ev & K. Roth (Eds.), *Education in the era of globalization* (pp. 123–146). Dordrecht: Springer.

Lukacs, G. (1971). *History and class consciousness: Studies in Marxist dialectics* (R. Livingstone, Trans). Cambridge, MA: MIT Press. (Original work published 1923.)

Lupart, J., Chmiliar, L., Grigg, N., & Hiebert, B. (2004). Campus Alberta: Inclusive/special education initiative. *Exceptionality Education Canada, 14* (2 & 3), 9–24.

Lyotard, J.-F. (1984). *The postmodern condition: A report on knowledge*. Manchester, England: University of Manchester Press.

MacIntyre, A. (1997). *After virtue: A study in moral theory*. Notre Dame, IN: University of Notre Dame Press.

Mak, M. (2006). Unwanted images: Tackling gender-baeed violence in South African schools through art work. In F. Leach and C. Mitchell (eds). Combating gender violence in and around schools. Stoke on Trent: Trentha,

Mak, M., Mitchell, C., & Stuart, J. (Writers) (2005). *Our photos, our videos, our stories: Addressing HIV and AIDS in the community* [Motion picture]. Canada: Taffeta Films.

Manitoba Education Administration Act, R.S.M. 1987, c. E10.

Manitoba Education and Training (1994). *Renewing Education: New Directions—A Blueprint for Action*. Winnipeg, Manitoba, Canada: Author.

Marginson, S. (2004). National and global competition in higher education. *The Australian Educational Researcher, 31* (2), 1–28.

Marginson, S. (2006). University leaders' strategies in the global environment: A comparative study of Universitas Indonesia and the Australian National University. *Higher Education, 52*, 343–373.

Marginson, S. (2007a). University mission and identity for a post-public era. *Higher Education Research and Development, 26* (1), 117–131.

Marginson, S. (2007b). The public/private division in higher education: A global revision. *Higher Education, 53*, 307–333.

Martin, J., Sugarman, J., & Thompson, J. (2003). *Psychology and the question of agency*. Albany: State University of New York Press.

Mason, J. (2002). *Researching your own practice: The discipline of noticing*. London: RoutledgeFalmer.

Mayhew, M. J., & Grunwald, H. E. (2006). Factors contributing to faculty incorporation of diversity-related course content. *The Journal of Higher Education 77* (1), 148–168.

Maynard, T. (1996). The limits of mentoring: The contribution of the higher education tutor to primary student teachers' school-based learning. In J. Furlong & R. Smith (Eds.), *The role of higher education in initial teacher training* (pp. 101-118). London: Kogan Page.

McCarthy, C. (1998) Educating the American popular: Suburban resentment and the representation of the inner city in contemporary film and television. *Race, Ethnicity, and Education 1* (1), 31–47.

McKay, A. (2004). Adolescent Sexual and Reproductive Health in Canada: A Report Card in 2004. *The Canadian Journal of Human Sexuality, 13*(2), 67-81.

McIntyre, D. J., & Byrd, D. M. (1998). In G. R. Firth & E. F. Pajak, (Eds.), *Handbook of Research on School Supervision* (pp. 409–427). New York: Macmillan.

McIntyre, J., Byrd, D., & Foxx, S. (1996). Field and laboratory experiences. In J. Sikula (Ed.), *Handbook of research on teacher education* (pp. 171–193). New York: Macmillan.

McWilliam, E. (2008). Making excellent teachers. In A. Phelan & J. Sumsion (Eds.), *Critical readings in teacher education: Provoking absences* (pp. 33–44). Rotterdam, The Netherlands: Sense Publishers.

Middlehurst, R. (2004). Changing internal governance: A discussion of leadership roles and management structures in U.K. universities. *Higher Education Quarterly, 58* (4), 258–279.

Miller, M. (2008, January). First, kill all the school boards. *Atlantic Monthly, 301*(1), 92–97. Retrieved October 28, 2008, from http://www.theatlantic.com/doc/200801/miller-education.

Ministère de l'Éducation (1994). *La formation à l'éducation préscolaire et à l'enseignement primaire. Orientations et compétences attendues.* Québec, Canada: Gouvernement du Québec.

Mitchell, C. (2006). Visual arts-based methodologies in research as social change. In T. Marcus (Ed.), *Shifting the boundaries of knowledge.* Scottsville, South Africa: University of KwaZulu-Natal Press.

Mitchell, C., & Smith, A. (2003). Sick of AIDS: Literacy and the meaning of life for South African youth. *Culture, Health & Sexuality, 5* (6), 513–522.

Mitchell, C., & Weber, S. (1999). *Reinventing ourselves as teachers: Beyond nostalgia.* London: Falmer Press.

Mitchell, C., & Weber, S. (2005). Just who do we think we are . . . and how do we know this? Re-visioning pedagogical spaces for studying our teaching selves. In C. Mitchell, S. Weber, & K. O'Reilly-Scanlon (Eds.), *Just who do we think we are? Methodologies for autobiography and self-study in teaching* (pp. 1–9). London: RoutledgeFalmer.

Mitchell, C., De Lange, N, Moletsane, R. Stuart, J, Buthelezi, T. & Taylor, M. (2005). Giving a face to HIV and AIDS: On the uses of photo-voice by teachers and community health care workers working with youth in rural South Africa. *Qualitative Research in Psychology 3* (2), 257-270.

Mitchell, C., De Lange, N., & Nguyen, T. (2008). Let's not leave this problem: Exploring emergent implementation discourses in inclusive education through the eyes of teachers as video producers in rural South Africa. *Prospects.*

Mitchell, C., Low, B., & Hoechsmann, M. (2006). Developing a webtool on arts-based and other partipatory approaches to HIV and AIDS education. Report to Culture and HIV, UNESCO, Paris.

Mitchell, C., Moletsane, R., & De Lange, N. (2007). Inclusive education in South Africa in the era of AIDS: Every voice counts. *International Journal of Inclusive Education 11* (4), 383–386.

Mitchell, C., Walsh, S., & Moletsane, R. (2006). Speaking for ourselves: A case for visual arts-based and other participatory methodologies in working with young people to address sexual violence. In F. Leach & C. Mitchell (Eds.), *Combating gender violence in and around schools*. London: Trentham Books.

Mitchell, C., Weber, S., & Pithouse, K. (in press). Facing the public: Using photography for self-study and social action. In D. Tidwell, M. Heston & L. Fitzgerald (Eds.), *Research methods for the self-study of practice*. New York: Springer.

Mitchell, C., Weber, S., & Yoshida, Y. (2008). Where are the youth in faculties of education? In A. Phelan (Ed.), *Provoking absences in teacher education*. Amsterdam: Sense.

Mitchell, C., Weber, S., & Pithouse, K. (2009). Facing the public: Using photography for self-study and social action. In D. Tidwell, M. Heston & L. Fitzgerald (Eds.), *Research methods for the self-study of practice*. New York: Springer. 98-110.

Mitchell, C., Weber, S., & Yoshida, R. (2008). Where are the youth?: Reframing teacher education within the context of youth participation. Anne Phelan & Jennifer Sumsion, *Critical readings in teacher education:Provoking absences*. Rotterdam: Sense Publishers. 139-154

Mitchell, C., De Lange, N, Moletsane, R., Stuart, J., Taylor, M. and Buthelezi, T. (in press). "Trust no one at school": Participatory video with young people in addressing gender violence in and around South African schools. In F. Ogunleye (ed.) *African Video Film Today 2*. Matsapha, Swaziland: Academic Publishers Swaziland.

Mitchell, M. F., & Schwager, S. (1993). Improving the student teaching experience: Looking to the research for guidance. *Physical Educator, 50* (1), 31–38.

Moletsane, R., De Lange, N., Mitchell, C., Stuart, J., Buthelezi, T., & Taylor, M. (2007). Photo-voice as a tool for analysis and activism in response to HIV and AIDS stigmatization in a rural KwaZulu-Natal school. *Journal of Child and Adolescent Mental Health, 19* (1), 19–28.

Moreno, J. M. (2007). Do the initial and continuous teachers' professional development prepare teachers to understand and cope with the complexities of today and tomorrow's world? *Journal of Educational Change, 8*, 169–173.

Morrell, R., & Makhaye, G. (2006). Working not blaming: Masculinity work with young African men in KwaZulu-Natal. In. F. Leach & C. Mitchell (Eds.), *Combating gender violence in and around schools* (pp. 153–162). London: Trentham.

Munby, H., & Russell, T. (1994). The authority of experience in learning to teach: Messages from a physics methods class. *Journal of Teacher Education, 4*, 86–95.

Murray, J., & Male, T. (2005). Becoming a teacher educator: Evidence from the field. *Teaching and Teacher Education, 21*, 125–142.

Myers, D., & Saul, D. (1974). How not to reform a teacher education system. In D. Myers & F. Reid, (Eds.), *Educating teachers: Critiques and proposals*. Toronto, Ontario, Canada: OISE Press.

Napoleoni, L. (2008). *Rogue economics*. London: Allen & Unwin.

National Commission on Excellence in Education (1983). *A nation at risk: The imperative for educational reform*. Washington, DC: U.S. Government Printing Office.

NCATE (2007, May). About NCATE. Retrieved November 2, 2008, from http://www.ncate.org/public/aboutNCATE.asp.

NCLB (2002). Public law 107–110—January 8, 2002. Retrieved November 2, 2008, from http://www.ed.gov/policy/elsec/leg/esea02/107-110.pdf.

NEA (n.d.). About NEA: The nation's largest professional employee organization. Retrieved November 2, 2008, from http://www.nea.org/ about-nea/index.html.

NEA (2008), *Rankings estimates*, NEA Research, Atlanta: Georgia, National Education Society, retrieved June 18, 2009 from http://www.nea.org/assets/docs/09rankings.pdf

NEA-AFT (2001). NEA-AFT partnership. Retrieved November 2, 2008, from http://www.nea.org/aboutnea/NEA-AFTPartnership.html.

Nevin, A., Cohen, J., Salazar, L., & Marshall, D. (2007, February). Student teacher perspectives on inclusive education. Paper presented at the Annual Conference of the American Association of Colleges of Teacher Education Strand IV, New York, NY.

Nikiforuk, A. (1993). *School's out: The catastrophe in public education and what we can do about it*. Toronto, Ontario, Canada: MacFarlane, Walter & Ross.

Noddings, N. (1992). *The challenge to care in schools: An alternative approach to education*. New York: Teachers College Press.

Noddings, N. (2002). *Educating moral people: A caring alternative to character education*. New York: Teachers College Press.
Normand-Guérette, D. (1998). La formation des enseignants associés. Des stratégies pour mieux les outiller dans leurs rôles d'enseignants et de formateurs. In D. Raymond & Y. Lenoir (Eds.), *Enseignants de métier et formation initiale* (pp. 103–122). Brussels, Belgium: DeBoeck.
Norris, G., Mbokasi, T., Rorke, F., Goba, S., & Mitchell, C. (2007). Where do we start? Using collage to explore very young adolescents' knowledge about HIV and AIDS in 4 senior primary classrooms in KwaZulu-Natal. *International Journal of Inclusive Education, 11* (4), 481–499.
Nozick, R. (1989). *The examined life: Philosophical meditations*. New York: Touchstone.
NPBEA (2002). Standards for Advanced Programs in Educational Leadership. Retrieved November 2, 2008 from http://www.npbea.org/ELCC/ELCCStandards%20_5-02.pdf.
O'Byrne, A. (2005). Pedagogy without a project: Arendt and Derrida on teaching, responsibility and revolution. *Studies in Philosophy and Education, 24*, 389–409.
OECD (2004). Learning for tomorrow's world: First results from PISA 2003, table 2.6, p. 358.
Ollman, B. (2003). *Dance of the dialectic: Steps in Marx's method*. Urbana: University of Illinois Press.
Olssen, M. (2000). Ethical liberalism, education and the "new right." *Journal of Education Policy, 15 (*5), 481–508.
Olssen, M., & Peters, M. (2005). Neoliberalism, higher education and the knowledge economy: From the free market to knowledge capitalism. *Journal of Education Policy, 20* (3), 313–345.
Organisation pour la coopération et le développement économique (OCDE). (2001). *L'école de demain: Quel avenir pour nos écoles?* Centre pour la recherche et l'innovation dans l'enseignement. Paris: Éditions OCDE.
Organisation pour la coopération et le développement économique (OCDE). (2005). *Le rôle crucial des enseignants. Attirer, former et retenir des enseignants de qualité*. Paris: Éditions OCDE.
Pakravan, P. (2006). *The future is not what it used to be: Reexamining postsecondary funding mechanisms in Canada*. Toronto, Ontario, Canada: C. D. Howe Institute.
Palmer, P. J. (1998). *The courage to teach: Exploring the inner landscape of a teacher's life*. San Francisco: Jossey-Bass.

Patrick, D., Wong, T., & Jordan, R. (2000). Sexually transmitted infections in Canada: Recent resurgence threatens national goals. *The Canadian Journal of Sexuality, 9*(3), 149-165.

Pattman, R. (2006). Making pupils the resources and promoting gender equality in HIV/AIDS. *Journal of Education, 38*, 89–116.

Pearson, P. D. (in press). An historical analysis of the impact of educational research on policy and practice: Reading as an illustrative case. In D. W. Rowe, R. Jimenez, D. Compton, D. Dickinson, Y. Kim, K. Leander, & V. Risko (Eds.), $56^{th}$ *National Reading Conference Yearbook* (pp. 1–30).

Pederson, K. G., & Fleming, T. (1979). The more things change, the more they stay the same: Some inescapable conclusions on the nature of teacher education. *Teacher Education, 14* (2), 40–49.

Petersen, B. (2006). Rethinking Teacher Unions. *Rethinking Schools, 20* (3). Retrieved from http://www.rethinkingschools.org/archive/20_03/20_03.shtml.

Phelan, A. (1996). Strange pilgrims: Nostalgia and disillusionment in teacher education reform. *Interchange, 27* (3 & 4), 331–348.

Phelan, A. (2001). Power and place in teaching and teacher education. *Journal of Teaching and Teacher Education: An International Journal of Research and Studies, 17* (5), 583–597.

Phelan, A. (2005). On discernment: The practice of wisdom and the wisdom of practice in teacher education. In Garry Hoban (Ed.), *The Missing Links in Teacher Education: Innovative Approaches in Designing Teacher Education Programs* (pp. 57-73). Netherlands: Kluwver Press.

Phelan, A., & Sumsion, J. (2008). Introduction: Lines of flight and lines of articulation in teacher education. In A. Phelan & J. Sumsion (Eds.), *Critical readings in teacher education: Provoking absences* (pp. 5–22). Rotterdam, The Netherlands: Sense Publishers.

Phillips, S. (2002). *Teacher quality in Canada* (SAEE Research Series # 12), Kelowna, BC, Canada: Society for the Advancement of Excellence in Education. Retrieved from: http://www.saee.ca/pdfs/9780968993675.pdf

Pinar, W. (2004). *Curriculum and study, not curriculum and teaching*. Unpublished manuscript.

Pithouse, K. (2007). *Learning through teaching: A narrative self-study of a novice teacher educator.* Unpublished doctoral thesis, University of KwaZulu-Natal, Durban, South Africa.

Porath, M., & Jordan, E. (2004). Problem-based learning in teacher education: Constructing knowledge of exceptionality. *Exceptionality Education Canada, 14* (2 & 3), 47–64.

# References

Postman, N., & Weingartner, C. (1969). *Teaching as a subversive activity.* New York: Delacorte Press.
Powers, E. (2006, June 6). A Spirited Disposition Debate, Inside Higher Ed. Retrieved November 2, 2008, from http://www.insidehighered.com/news/2006/06/06/disposition.
President discusses global war on terror. (2006, September 5). *The Globe and Mail.*
Public Health Agency of Canada. (2006). HIV/AIDS Epi Updates. Retrieved November 8th, 2007, from http://www.phacaspc.gc//publicat/epiu-aepi/epi-06/index.html
Public Health Agency of Canada. (2007). HIV/AIDS Epi Updates, November 2007. In *Surveillance and Risk Assessment Division, Centre for Disease Prevention and Control*: Public Heatlh Agency of Canada.
Raptis, H., & Fleming, T. (2003). *Reframing education: How to create effective schools.* Toronto, Ontario, Canada: C. D. Howe Institute.
Readings, B. (1996). *The university in ruins.* Cambridge, MA: Harvard University Press.
Rikard, G. L., & Veal, M. L. (1996). Cooperating teachers : Insight into their preparation, beliefs, and practices. *Journal of Teaching in Physical Education, 15,* 279–296.
Rotermann, M. (2005). Sex, condoms and STDs among young people. *Health Reports, 16*(3), 39-45 (Statistics Canada Catalogue no. 82-003).
Rothstein, R. (2000). Equalizing education resources on behalf of disadvantaged children, in R. D. Kahlenberg (Ed.), *A notion at risk: Preserving public education as an engine for social mobility* (pp. 31-92). New York: Century.
Russell, T. (1997). Teaching teachers: How I teach is the message. In J. Loughran & T. Russell (Eds.), *Teaching about teaching: Purpose, passion and pedagogy in teacher education* (pp. 32–47). London: Falmer Press.
Russell, T., & Korthagen, F. (Eds.) (1995). *Teachers who teach teachers: Reflections on teacher education.* London: Falmer Press.
Russell, T., & Loughran, J. (Eds.) (2007). *Enacting a pedagogy of teacher education: Values, relationships and practices.* London: Routledge.
Sapon-Shevin, M., & Zollers, N .J. (1999). Multicultural and disability agendas in teacher education: Preparing teachers for diversity. *International Journal of Leadership in Education, 2* (3), 165–190.
Schön, D.A. (1987). *Educating the reflective practitioner: Towards a new design for teaching and learning in the professions.* San Francisco: Jossey-Bass.

Schön, D.A. (1988) Coaching reflective teaching. In P. P. Grimmett & G. L. Erickson (Eds.), *Reflection in teacher education* (pp. 19–29). New York: Teachers College Press.

Sheehan, N., & Fullan, M. (1995). Teacher education in Canada: A case study of British Columbia and Ontario. In M. F. Wideen & P.P. Grimmett (Eds.), *Changing times in teacher education: Restructuring or reconceptualizing?* (pp. 89–102). London: Falmer Press.

Shields, C. M. (2009), *Courageous leadership for transforming schools: Democratizing practice*. Norwood, MA: Christopher-Gordon.

Slaughter, S., & Leslie, L. (1997). *Academic capitalism: Politics, policies, and the entrepreneurial university*. Baltimore: Johns Hopkins University Press.

Smits, H. (2008, May). Invited panel on teacher education: Crossing borders in teacher education curriculum. Paper presented at the Canadian Society for Studies in Education Conference, Vancouver, BC, Canada.

Smyth, J., & Shacklock, G. (1998). *Re-making teaching: Ideology, policy and practice*. London: Routledge.

Stallybrass, P., & White, A. (1986). *The politics and poetics of transgression*. London: Methuen.

Street, B. (1984). *Literacy in theory and practice*. Cambridge, England: Cambridge University Press.

Stuart J. (2007). From our frames: Exploring with teachers the pedagogic possibilities of a visual arts-based approach to HIV and AIDS. *Journal of Education, 38 (3)*, 67–88.

Stuart J. (2006). From our frames: Exploring with teachers the pedagogic possibilities of a visual arts-based approach to HIV and AIDS. Unpublished doctoral dissertation, University of KwaZulu-Natal, South Africa.

Stuart, J. (2004). Media matters: Producing a culture of compassion in the age of AIDS. *English Quarterly, 36* (2), 3–5.

Stuart, J., & Mitchell, C. (2007, June). Where are the youth in faculties of education? Preservice teachers as cultural producers in addressing HIV and AIDS. Fourteenth International Teaching and Learning Conference, Wits University, Johannesburg, South Africa.

Talvitie, U., Peltokallio, L., & Männistö, P. (2000). Student teachers' views about their relationships with university supervisors, cooperating teachers and peer student teachers. *Scandinavian Journal of Educational Research*, *44* (1), 79–88.

Tardif, M., & Lessard, C. (1999). *Le travail enseignant au quotidien: expérience, interactions humaines et dilemmes professionnels*. Québec: Presses de l'Université Laval.

Timmons, V. (2006). Impact of a multipronged approach to inclusion: Having all partners on side. *International Journal of Inclusive Education, 10*, 469–480.

Trier, J. (2001a). The cinematic representation of the personal and professional lives of teachers. *Teacher Education Quarterly, 28* (3), 127–142.

Trier, J. (2001b). Challenging the cinematic construction of literacy with preservice teachers. *Teaching Education, 12* (3), 301–314.

Trier, J. (2002). Exploring the concept of habitus with preservice teachers through the use of popular school films. *Interchange: A Quarterly Review of Education, 33* (3), 237–260.

Trier, J. (2003). Inquiring into techniques of power with preservice teachers through the school film *The Paper Chase. Teaching and Teacher Education, 19* (5), 543–557.

Trier, J. (2005). Sordid fantasies: Reading popular culture inner city school films as racialized texts with pre-service teachers. *Race, Ethnicity and Education, 8*(2), 171–189.

Trier, J. (2006a). Reconceptualizing literacy through a discourses perspective by analyzing literacy events represented in films about schools. *Journal of Adolescent and Adult Literacy, 49* (6), 510–523.

Trier, J. (2006b). Teaching with media and popular culture. *Journal of Adolescent and Adult Literacy, 49* (5), 434–438.

Trier, J. (2007). Cool engagements with YouTube: Part 1. *Journal of Adolescent and Adult Literacy, 50* (5), 408–412.

Trier, J. (in press). *The 400 Blows* as cinematic literacy narrative. *Teacher Education Quarterly.*

UNAIDS. (2006). *Report on the global HIV/AIDS epidemic: Executive summary.* Retrieved from http: data.unaids.org/pub/Global Report/2006.

UNESCO (1994). The UNESCO Salamanca statement and framework for action on special needs education. Paris: UNESCO.

United Nations Committee on the Rights of Persons with Disabilities (2006). *Convention on the Rights of Persons with Disabilities.* Geneva: UNCRPD. Retrieved January 15, 2008, from http://www.un.org/disabilities/default.asp?navid=12&pid=150.

U.S. Department of Education. (n.d.) ED.gov. Retrieved October 27, 2008, from http://www.ed.gov/about/landing.jhtml?src=gu,

U.S. DOE (2007). Free appropriate public education for students with disabilities: Requirements under section 504 of the Rehabilitation Act of 1973. U.S. Department of Education Office for Civil Rights, Washington, DC., 20202, September 2007. Retrieved November 2, 2008, from http://www.ed.gov/about/offices/list/ocr/docs/edlite-FAPE504.html.

Van Manen, M. (1977). Linking ways of knowing with ways of being practical. *Curriculum Inquiry, 6* (3), 205–228.
Verstegen, D. A. (2007). Has adequacy been achieved? A study of finances and costs a decade after court ordered reform. *Journal of Education Finance, 32* (3), 304–327.
Verstegen, D. A., & Driscoll, L. G. (2008). Educational opportunity: The Illinois dilemma, *Journal of Education Finance, 33* (4), 331–351.
Villa, D. (1997). Hannah Arendt: Modernity, alienation and aritique. In C. Calhoun & J. McGowen (Eds.), *Hannah Arendt and the meaning of politics* (pp. 179–206). Minneapolis, MN: University of Minneapolis Press.
Villegas, A., & Lucas, T. (2002). Preparing culturally responsive teachers: Rethinking the curriculum. *Journal of Teacher Education, 53,* 20–33.
Walsh, S. (Writer), & Mitchell, C (Producer). (2004). *Fire & Hope* [Motion picture]. Canada: Taffeta Films.
Walsh, S., & Mitchell, C. (2006). "I'm too young to die": Danger, desire and masculinity in the neighbourhood. *Gender and Development 14* (1), 57–68.
Wasley, P. (2006, June 6). Accreditor of education schools drops controversial "social justice" language. *Chronicle of Higher Education, 52* (41), A13. Retrieved November 2, 2008, from http://nameorg.org/pipermail/name-mce_nameorg.org/2006-June/000990.html.
Wasley, P. A., & McDiarmid, G. W. (2003, July). Tying the assessment of new teachers to student learning and to teacher preparation. Paper prepared for the 2003 National Commission on Teaching and America's Future Meeting. Retrieved April 3, 2007, from http://www.nctaf.org/strategies/assure/quality_teacher_preparation/assessment_of_new_teachers.htm.
Wikipedia (2008). School districts. Retrieved October 26, 2008, from http://en.wikipedia.org/wiki/School_district.
Wiles, J., & Bondi, J. (2000). *Supervision: A guide to practice* (5th edition). Columbus, OH: Merrill.
Williams, A. (1994). Roles and responsibilities in initial teacher training: Student views. In A. Williams (Ed.) *Perspectives on partnership: Secondary initial teacher training* (pp. 93-108). London: Falmer Press.
Williams, J. D. (Ed.) (2002). *Vulnerable children.* Edmonton, Canada: University of Alberta Press.
Wingrove, E. (2007). [Review of the book *Feminism and the abyss of freedom.*] *Politics and Gender, 3*(3), 409–413.
Young, J., & Grimmett, P. P. (2008, June). Reconstructing the governance of initial teacher education in Canada: Recent developments in BC and

Manitoba. Paper presented at the annual conference of the Canadian Society for the Study of Education, Vancouver, BC, Canada.
Young, J., Hall, C., & Clarke, A. (2007). Challenges to university autonomy in initial teacher education programmes: The cases of England, Manitoba, and British Columbia. *Teaching and Teacher Education, 23* (1), 81–93.
Zeichner, K. (2006). Different conceptions of teacher expertise and teacher education in the U.S.A. *Education Research and Perspectives, 33* (2), 60–79.
Zeichner, K. M. (1995). Beyond the divide of teacher research and academic research. *Teachers and Teaching: Theory and Practice, 1*, 153–172.
Zeichner, K. M. (2005). Becoming a teacher educator: A personal perspective. *Teaching and Teacher Education, 21*, 117–124.
Zizek, S. (1992a). *Looking awry: An introduction to Jacques Lacan through popular culture*. Cambridge, MA: MIT Press.
Zizek, S. (1992b). *Everything you always wanted to know about Lacan but were afraid to ask Hitchcock*. New York: Verso.
Zizek, S. (2002). *Enjoy your symptom! Jacques Lacan in Hollywood and out*. New York: Routledge.
Zizek, S. (2006). *The Parallax view*. Cambridge, MA: The MIT Press.

## Studies in the Postmodern Theory of Education

*General Editors*
*Joe L. Kincheloe & Shirley R. Steinberg*

Counterpoints publishes the most compelling and imaginative books being written in education today. Grounded on the theoretical advances in criticalism, feminism, and postmodernism in the last two decades of the twentieth century, Counterpoints engages the meaning of these innovations in various forms of educational expression. Committed to the proposition that theoretical literature should be accessible to a variety of audiences, the series insists that its authors avoid esoteric and jargonistic languages that transform educational scholarship into an elite discourse for the initiated. Scholarly work matters only to the degree it affects consciousness and practice at multiple sites. Counterpoints' editorial policy is based on these principles and the ability of scholars to break new ground, to open new conversations, to go where educators have never gone before.

For additional information about this series or for the submission of manuscripts, please contact:

> Joe L. Kincheloe & Shirley R. Steinberg
> c/o Peter Lang Publishing, Inc.
> 29 Broadway, 18th floor
> New York, New York 10006

To order other books in this series, please contact our Customer Service Department:
> (800) 770-LANG (within the U.S.)
> (212) 647-7706 (outside the U.S.)
> (212) 647-7707 FAX

Or browse online by series:
> www.peterlang.com

www.ingramcontent.com/pod-product-compliance
Ingram Content Group UK Ltd.
Pitfield, Milton Keynes, MK11 3LW, UK
UKHW021838210426
5322IPUK00021B/357